OPPORTUNITIES IN
DESKTOP
PUBLISHING
CAREERS

Kenny Schiff

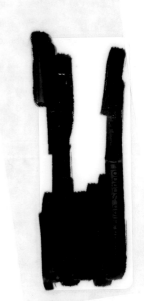

 **VGM Career Horizons**
a division of *NTC Publishing Group*
Lincolnwood, Illinois USA

Cover Photo Credits:

Front cover: upper left, upper right,
and lower left, Apple Computers;
lower right, DeVry, Inc.

Back cover: upper and lower left,
Apple Computers, upper right, DeVry Inc.

Library of Congress Cataloging-in-Publication Data

Schiff, Kenny.
    Opportunities in desktop publishing careers / Kenny Schiff.

      p.   cm. — (VGM opportunities series)
    Includes bibliographical references.
    ISBN 0-8442-4064-8 (hardcover) — ISBN 0-8442-4065-6
  (softcover)
      1. Desktop publishing—United States—Vocational guidance.
  I. Title. II. Series.
Z253.53.S34   1993
686.2'2544023'73—dc20   92-37882
                                                          CIP

ABOUT THE AUTHOR

Kenny Schiff is a writer, editor, desktop publisher, and teacher with a keen interest in technology. Like many of the individuals he profiles in *Opportunities in Desktop Publishing,* he came to desktop publishing through a circuitous route. And like many of his peers, he has been able to bring together many different interests and abilities in desktop publishing. Schiff is one of a new breed of professionals who integrate the work of several different specialties.

Since graduating from State University of New York's College at Oneonta in 1981, Schiff has worked as a musician, high school writing instructor, newspaper columnist, managing editor, college literature instructor, and technical writer. He received his M.S. in Education from St. John's University in 1985.

Schiff's first rudimentary attempts at desktop publishing came with a teachers' newsletter he coedited with a friend. Since then he has gone on to desktop-publish 14 full-length books, plus technical manuals, advertisements, brochures, direct-mail advertising pieces, and business forms.

Currently he is using his writing, editing, teaching, and desktop publishing background as a trainer for an educational technology company in the Chicago area, where he lives with his wife, Jennifer, and their cat, Harley.

FOREWORD

Publishing. Once the realm of grand houses and powerful newspapers. But today the computer has put publishing within reach of every individual with fresh ideas and unique insight. Desktop publishing has exploded into a world of numerous opportunities and unlimited potential. For the businessperson, publisher, graphic artist, freelancer, or entrepreneur, desktop publishing is an indispensable skill. If your ambitions run in either of these veins, challenges await you. Your imagination, expertise, and hard work will be welcome in this field.

Good luck as you explore the many and diverse career paths offered in desktop publishing.

The Editors
VGM Career Books

CONTENTS

INTRODUCTION

As you will learn in the pages of this book, desktop publishing (DTP)[1] is a new and exciting area to work in. But if you could go back in time a few years and drop the phrase at a party, at school, or among businesspeople, you would get blank stares. Though DTP today is an everyday part of the computer, business, publishing, and art world, prior to 1985 it did not exist.

As with many new techniques and technologies, DTP came upon us fast and spread even faster. With this growth came an entirely new set of jobs for individuals with varying degrees of training and experience. Scan your local yellow pages and you'll find many different businesses that specialize in this field. Browse your local paper's Sunday classified section and you'll find jobs in areas as diverse as

---

[1]The common abbreviation for desktop publishing is DTP. For the sake of continuity, subsequent references to desktop publishing may use this accepted abbreviated form.

advertising, marketing, engineering, secretarial, graphic art, publishing, and education that involve using DTP, either as a major part of the job description or as a small component. Whether you choose to pursue DTP as an area to specialize in or whether you have interest in it as a component of your job, opportunities abound.

The pages of this book will introduce you to all kinds of businesses and individuals who use DTP to communicate with the world. At the heart of this book are the words and thoughts of actual desktop publishers. In their own voices they will tell you all about their work and let you know what kinds of opportunities exist for someone like yourself. But before we go further, let's examine what DTP is.

CHAPTER 1

WHAT IS DESKTOP PUBLISHING?

Though no official story exists on its origin, the term *desktop publishing,* or *DTP,* is generally thought to have been coined in 1985 by Paul Brainerd, then president of Seattle's Aldus Corporation. Aldus had just developed a revolutionary new software program, PageMaker, the first commercially available computer application that brought together and utilized the new potential of Apple's new Macintosh computers and their newly developed Laser-Writer printer. The forward-thinking Brainerd knew that his product and the others that would soon be introduced would open publishing possibilities to literally millions of new people. No longer would publishing be controlled by corporations and large printing houses, nor would one need to invest in gargantuan, hard-to-use equipment. Publishing had become mobile. It could now take place on your desktop, and—perhaps even more revolutionary—sometimes that desktop would be in your home.

MAKING PAGES

Borrowing the page-making concept from graphic arts, PageMaker allowed someone who owned a laser printer and a personal computer to design and print high-quality, camera-ready pages. Because it allowed a user to mix graphic images and text on the page, it was the first software package that freed the graphic designer, writer, or printer from having to utilize pasteup (literally pasting photographs or artwork onto a page). PageMaker allowed the user for the first time to compose pages right on a computer screen. This new ability to preview the printed page on the computer screen came to be known as What-You-See-Is-What-You-Get (WYSIWYG).

The development of Apple's LaserWriter and Hewlett Packard's LaserJet printers boosted the printing quality available for the personal computer. No longer were computer users having to settle for poor-quality dot-matrix printouts, or wait on the painfully slow daisy-wheel printers of the day. Now they had the relative sharpness of typeset documents, and the flexibility of proportional typefaces. The average writer, graphic artist, or small-business operator now had the option to select literally hundreds of typefaces that were up until that point only available to professional printers and people with expensive typesetting equipment.

The PageMaker/Macintosh/LaserWriter combination was the first real DTP setup, but it only scratched the surface of what was to become available to desktop publishers in the next few years. Xerox's Ventura Publisher came next in 1986, opening up DTP for users of IBM-style computers. Where PageMaker worked from the page up, Ventura automated the process of making books, allowing for a new generation of snazzy technical documentation and seamlessly generated books. And there were many others to follow.

IBM-style computers were cheaper to manufacture than Apple computers, and during the mid 1980s, they saw unprecedented growth. While many artists chose the Macintosh, many businesses wanted to build off of their investment in IBM-style computers and use their growing publishing capabilities. This potent combination of a large supply of powerful computers, high-quality laser printers, and sophisticated, user-friendly software made millions of users capable of producing professional-looking publications.

A DEFINITION

What defines DTP, and makes it so revolutionary, is that an author, artist, office worker, or small-business owner can use it to create and produce reader-ready work without needing the services of outside professionals. DTP equipment can fit in a relatively compact space and can be had for a relatively inexpensive price.

DTP gives the user access to a high-quality set of graphic tools, allowing him or her to build, enhance, and translate ideas, concepts, and thoughts. With the use of drawing programs, devices like scanners, libraries of clip art and photographs, and an endless variety of typefaces and symbols (some not available even to traditional printers), the desktop publisher can assemble exciting pages that enhance and build off of the information they contain. DTP offers an unprecedented amount of control over one's own work.

In the 1990s we take this ability for granted, but we have come far in a short time. In order to really understand the impact of DTP, let's take a brief side trip back through history. Let's look at how publishing and printing developed so that you can see where DTP started, where it's going, and where you can fit into it.

CHAPTER 2

A HISTORY OF PRINTED WORDS

In the beginning there was the spoken word. No CNN, no faxed newsletters, no direct-mail advertising, no slick magazines, no newspapers, no books. Stories got passed down by word of mouth. History was passed on mother to daughter, father to son.

Later, aspiring cave artists, the graffiti makers of the prehistoric day, put their messages on cave walls. But it was difficult to move cave walls around, so these early communicators couldn't reach a very large audience. It was left to their family and neighbors to enjoy their latest masterpiece.

Eventually, these would-be journalists, novelists, and graphic artists hungered for larger audiences and permanence. They began to write on more portable materials like clay and stone.

Time brought ingenuity and improvement. Communicators began to put their messages on processed animal skins. Around the second century B.C. the people of Pergamum (modern-day Turkey) helped develop parchment as the medium for the written word. Parchment and vellum scrolls were both lightweight and durable—better than cave walls, but there was still no method of mass reproduction. And it was painfully slow to produce even one document. Imagine how long it might take a writer to laboriously transcribe, letter by neat letter, even one version of the Old Testament—and without White Out^{TM}!

A larger problem was that almost everyone was illiterate, so no matter how fast scribes and monks in Europe could reproduce religious or legal texts, few could read what was written. Things remained that way until the Middle Ages.

The forces of change were slow. Organized calligraphers and church officials worked hard to restrict methods of duplication. They liked the fact that they were the only ones who could read and write and they wanted to keep it that way. The eventual development of mechanical means of reproducing words took centuries to emerge. And when it did happen, it was revolutionary. It would turn out to be the development that would bring about the freedom and the literacy that we expect today.

PAPER AND MOVABLE TYPE

The Chinese are credited with inventing paper and movable wooden type. However, their complex pictographic alphabet required hundreds and thousands of subtly different letters and made mass-production impress printing (like a rubber stamp) difficult, if not impossible, to accomplish.

It wasn't until about 1440, when German goldsmith Johannes Gutenberg developed movable metal type, that printing began to expand beyond a very small scale. His press, adapted from a cheese or wine press, could print about 300 sheets a day. There is speculation that others had experimented with this type of reproduction, but it took Gutenberg's fine work to firmly establish printing as a medium for communication. His work set a standard that was to last hundreds of years. Gutenberg's printing of Bibles was extraordinarily good, even by today's standards. And this new ability to reproduce the written word via a printing press was a major factor in bringing Europe out of the dark ages. Now ideas could be easily and inexpensively shared.

LETTERPRESS

The first few hundred years of the printing business were not an easy go. Composing type required careful and precise effort that was extremely time-consuming. The individual letters had to be selected by hand and placed into a frame one by one. This process was called letterpress, a method that is still used in economically underdeveloped countries. If you consider that this small book you're reading contains approximately 50,000 words, each word approximately six letters, that checks in at about 300,000 letters. Early letterpress printers would spend weeks and months setting the text for one book. Additions or revisions would further complicate the process, and some books required years to produce.

Ottmar Mergenthaler, a German-American inventor, during the 1880s brought printing into the modern age with his development of the Linotype machine, but the ability to manipulate text (words) and graphics (pictures) was still the work of a professional printer and a very specialized process. Mergenthaler's machine overcame the problems of the earlier letterpress—it put together words a line at a time, saving printers time and money—but still the distance between the creator of a book, pamphlet, magazine, or document was several layers away from the person who actually produced it for final reproduction. Documents could take months to be produced. Books could sometimes take years to turn around, often making the information that they contained out of date by the time it was printed.

Newer printing techniques enabled revisions or changes and allowed for variation in style and format. Still, each additional person involved in the process added another potential element of error. Each additional person involved in the chain also added time and money to the job. Turnaround was still slow and inaccuracy was common.

Book and magazine publishers built this lag into their process and pricing structure, but there were many others who relied on the printed word who were looking for a way to retain control over their communication while attaining professional results.

THE TYPEWRITER

The emergence of the typewriter in the late 1800s was the first step in overcoming this inefficient process. Hard to believe that those clunky old Remington typewriters were a revolution for the written word, but for the first time in history someone who was not a printer or calligrapher could produce a document in a standardized format that was of high enough quality to present to others.

Typewriters of that day were rather crude compared to even the simplest office machine of today, but they did the trick. So forward was the thinking behind their production that they remained relatively unchanged for almost a century. In fact, the QWERTY-style keyboard (named after the alphabetic letters that sit together on the keyboard's second row) is a direct descendant of those initial machines.

Typewriting was limited. Corrections were difficult to make. It was impossible to justify text—that is, to line up the margins so that they were flush on both the left and right side like this book. Except for using messy carbon paper, you could only make one copy at a time. But things started to change.

Soon there came some relatively inexpensive means of reproduction. In the 1930s came the mimeograph machine, which allowed typewriter users the ability to prepare masters that could be reproduced without using the services of a professional printer. Then in the 1950s came the first Xerox machines which gave every office and school the ability to photocopy and distribute its work.

These advances made it possible for writers and businesses to produce good quality work, and to reproduce their printed documents on a large scale at a relatively inexpensive price. Yet an individual or business that wanted to distribute anything of higher quality, with a more sophisticated presentation, one that perhaps included both text and graphics, still had to utilize the often expensive services of an outside professional.

WORD PROCESSING AND COMPUTERIZED TYPESETTING

In the mid-1960s, the first word-processing machinery appeared, which allowed the possibility of storing information for later retrieval. These machines allowed a writer to save her or his work so that she or he might be able to come back to it later and change it. It also marked the beginning of what would later become desktop publishing. Information became easily stored, retrieved, revised, and reproduced. The equipment was very expensive and still was not able to deliver much in the way of style or format, but it marked the beginnings of major changes in the office environment. It began the shift toward shorter turnaround times and more user control. These machines helped to put together and reproduce the enormous amount of information that was now available to even the smallest business. No longer would secretaries have to retype entire documents for corrections or additions. Often this material could be transferred electronically to a printer's professional typesetting equipment and transformed into a final form.

In the magazine, book, and newspaper industries, changes were also beginning at a rapid rate. They, too, were beginning to utilize new technologies to produce their publications. The Linotype machine that Mergenthaler developed remained the predominant method of reproduction until the 1950s. Linotype produced high-quality results but was a difficult and dangerous process, requiring printers to melt lead in order to set lines of type.

In the late 1950s and early 1960s the first computerized typesetting equipment came into use. It allowed printers to utilize cathode-ray tube monitors (CRTs) and keyboards to set type for publication. Now they, too, could store, retrieve, revise, and reproduce information in an automated fashion. Quality improved and turnaround time decreased.

PHOTOENGRAVING AND SCREENING

Prior to the development of photographic technology in the 1800s, any time a graphic image (picture) needed to be reproduced for publication, it needed first to be transformed into a woodcut—a time-consuming and expensive process. That changed with the development of photoengraving, which allowed printers to take an image and make a printing plate from it by exposing a specially treated metal sheet to light. By placing a very coarse screen above this plate, before it was exposed to light, the printer would produce a halftone, the same kind of image that is now found in newspapers and books.

If you look closely at the images in this book or in today's newspaper, you will see that the graphic images are made up of patterns of tiny dots. This same concept is utilized in computers and DTP in bit-mapped computer graphics, where pictures are reproduced from their patterns of dots. Look closely at the picture that your Nintendo machine produces or that you see at a video arcade or on your school's computer screen—they are also made up of dots. With the advent and improvement of screening techniques, printers could easily integrate high-quality pictures and text into their finished work. Still there lacked a way for someone other than a printing professional to easily integrate words and pictures into the documents she or he was producing.

TECHNOLOGY BRINGS A CROSSOVER

With all this wonderful technology, the average businessperson with publishing needs or the small-time graphic artist still was dependent on the printer to put his or her message into a more finalized print form. Up until the early 1980s, there was very little, if any, crossover between industries or jobs. Writers wrote, illustrators illustrated, editors edited, designers designed, secretaries typed letters, and printers printed.

Perhaps it was an easier time. Individuals had a specific role, a certain set of skills that they learned and put to use in a logical fashion. In the short decade since computer giants Apple and IBM revolutionized the way we deal with information, words, and pictures with their introduction of the personal computer, life has changed drastically for office workers.

Now individuals at all levels, often without any special training in design or print production, can be expected to create, design, and reproduce documents of varying degrees of complexity—everything from a flyer announcing an afternoon meeting, to a company newsletter, to an annual report, to an advertisement in the local newspaper.

Sounds like there's a lot sitting on the shoulders of the average worker of the 90s. But as we will explore in the rest of the chapters of this book, personal computers have opened a lot of doors for the average person. The technology has allowed unprecedented access to the printed word.

It has allowed the creation of new kinds of jobs, and it has taken the drudgery out of many old jobs. Ask anyone who has had to manually address envelopes for a 5,000-piece mailing about what having a computer has done for the job. Or ask a publisher who needs to make revisions in the upcoming edition of a new directory what benefit DTP has had.

The work world that we will explore in the remaining pages of *Opportunities in Desktop Publishing* is one that is exciting and allows for enormous creative opportunities. Now let's find out about what you can do with DTP.

CHAPTER 3

WHERE THE JOBS ARE

Looking for a position as a desktop publisher, or one that contains a DTP component, requires some detective work. The jobs are there in abundance, but they are often tucked away in specialized areas. As you go about the job-search process, you will need to know what to look for and where to look. This section surveys some of the areas that are likely to contain opportunities. It will give you a sense of what categories the jobs can be found in, what the positions are called, and what kinds of background and expertise they require.

As an overview, the following tables bring together actual job listings advertised in the classified section of a large midwestern city that were collected over a six-week period. The later section of this book will go into more detail about each of these kinds of jobs.

The next few pages separate the listings by the headings that they were found under in the classified section. Sometimes this is by job title, like *graphic artist,* but sometimes the heading is more generic, like *administration*. The second column in the table is devoted to the actual listing as you would find it in the newspaper. Finally, a notes column gives further explanation or clarification about the job.

Table 3.1 Job Listings

Heading	Description	Notes
Word Processor	Heavy experience in WP 5.1, Lotus/Impress and Ventura.	This job involves not only some DTP, but also is a notch above being a straight typist. You would be preparing materials for smaller-scale reproduction.
Administrative	Area firm seeks organized individual to coordinate and maintain sales & marketing projects. Strong typing and PC skills required. Desktop publishing experience a plus. We offer excellent salary and benefits.	Not a heavy design or graphic orientation for this, but the individual hired for this position would be required to produce materials of presentation quality.
Graphic Arts TYPESETTER	For small graphic arts studio that produces catalogs and direct mail promotions. Must be experienced in Quark Xpress, Freehand and Photoshop on Macintosh workstation and troubleshoot computer problems.	The job calls for someone who is comfortable working with materials that others have designed and specified.
Desktop Publishing Specialist ARTIST	Association seeks creative individual with excellent knowledge of PageMaker on IBM PC systems. Good typing important. Familiarity with Windows, Multimate and Scan Jet software important. Keyline and pasteup as well as graphic design needed.	Job requires the production of materials that others have produced. Graphic/design orientation necessary, though not a heavily creative position.

Heading	Description	Notes
Graphic Artist	Seeking a creative individual with a college degree in graphic design and at least 3–5 years of recent experience. We require desktop publishing software experience, including PageMaker, Corel Draw and Quark. Responsibilities include the design and production of corporate communications materials from concept to camera-ready artwork. This is a fast-paced creative environment requiring the ability to work independently and handle simultaneous projects. Knowledge of printing techniques and technology is essential as this individual will work with printers on job specifications regarding layout, design and deadlines.	A job that synthesizes the more traditional role of the graphic artist and new technology. Not only does the individual design, but also produce materials.
Design COMPUTER GRAPHICS SPECIALIST	Ad agency is seeking a computer graphic specialist for its art studio. Candidates should have a design and production background and must be dependable, enthusiastic, willing to work overtime, possess superior skills and be proficient using Quark, Illustrator and Photoshop. Prepress knowledge a plus. Responsibilities include: layout, pasteup, typesetting, electronic keylines, and design.	This position builds on the more traditional graphic artist and combines production and design.

Heading	Description	Notes
Public Relations COMMUNICA-TIONS REP	Communications department of a major social service agency seeks individual with degree in journalism, public relations, English or related field to handle media relations, internal communications, and public affairs activities. Ability to plan and manage time to meet deadlines a must. Wordperfect, desktop publishing and basic photography helpful.	Desktop publishing is only a sideline to this job, but the individual would be required in certain situations to produce materials suitable for presentation and reproduction. This might include press releases, advertisements, and in-house publications.
Advertising	All-around advertising/catalog production assistant. Desktop publishing background required.	
Desktop Publisher	Expanding company seeks PageMaker/Quark expert.	These people are looking for someone who really knows a software package. If you already have experience with one desktop publishing software package, another won't be that difficult to learn. If you already have some DTP experience, it is not a bad idea to learn additional software. Temporary agencies often cross-train people for free once you register with them.

Heading	Description	Notes
Artist DESKTOP PUBLISHER	Progressive publishing company seeks a desktop publisher with graphic arts skills. Must be able to produce a variety of sales promotion and publication materials using Macintosh desktop publishing system. Bachelor's degree with an emphasis on graphic design. Extensive knowledge of software programs including PageMaker, Illustrator, Freehand, Persuasion.	This company's requirements are pretty straightforward. As with many positions that involve DTP, this company is looking for somebody who is versatile and adaptable. It won't be enough to just know software; you will need to have a design orientation, too.
Public Relations	Excellent opportunity for creative, organized individual in public relations department of major hospital. Responsibilities include developing and creating advertising, media relations, publications, and special events. Background should include exposure or experience with newspapers, radio and television advertising, and desktop publishing.	Not a position that is strictly DTP, and for many this is a plus. Here the DTP component is small, and just an enhancement to the rest of the position's responsibilities. A perfect opportunity to combine different skills and interests.
Editor	Editor with experience with magazine production needed. Knowledge of desktop publishing, graphics, layout, dummies, cover development and editing important.	A similar position, but this one is in the magazine field. Most magazines have gone to DTP, so if you're interested in magazines, it is an important skill, whether you're a writer, editor, or part of the production staff.

Heading	Description	Notes
Typesetter	Desktop publishing operator must know PageMaker, Quark and have traditional typesetting background. This is a production-level job.	One of the few DTP positions that isn't hidden away in the classified ads. Here you wouldn't be creating the materials, but literally producing. Not necessarily a creative position— you'd be putting into print materials that others have designed and created.
Printing	Desktop color area. Background in color stripping and desktop publishing necessary.	Traditional printers were initially slow to acquire desktop publishing technology, but now they must in order to compete. This organization is one in transition, and they're looking for someone who is comfortable with both the old and the new.
Production	Law firm seeks an individual to assist in the production tasks for the firm's wide variety of materials. Ideal candidate will have a working knowledge of desktop publishing, production and design experience, editing and proofreading capability, and strong communications skills.	This firm needs someone to help put its document into print. DTP is only part of the job, and this is a position that calls for versatility.

Heading	Description	Notes
Desktop Publishing Service Bureau Coordinator	Full service pre-press firm needs production person with 1–2 years service bureau experience. Advanced output and troubleshooting skills required. Emphasis on Quark applications.	Pre-press and service bureaus (covered later in this book) are the real workhorses of the desktop publishing business. Organizations hire them to carry out their production work so that they don't have to maintain the expense of having their own in-house facilities. An opportunity to work on a wide range of documents and materials.

CHAPTER 4

THE BUSINESS PUBLISHER

Today more and more businesses have taken their publishing needs in-house. Rather than rely on outside contractors who add time and expense to their projects that require typesetting and graphic enhancement, companies now rely on desktop publishing technology and their own in-house office staff to carry out many of the tasks that were once sent outside.

The sophistication of business publishing varies from company to company, often from department to department. In some organizations, the work might not be anything more than fancy word processing that uses proportional typefaces, multicolumn texts, or simple charts, tables, and graphs. This work might be carried out by administrative assistants or secretaries and might be only a small component of their job description. Other situations might call for sophisticated page layout and graphic design presentations that require trained professionals with an eye for design.

Because businesses of the '90s have substantial publishing requirements, tremendous opportunities exist in this segment of the DTP market. Whether you would like to join a company as a design professional who puts together proposals, in-house newsletters, and sophisticated presentations, or whether you would like to be a supporting player who dabbles in desktop publishing reports and everyday communications, this area shows great promise. This section will explore business publishers at several different levels. Let's start with office support staff.

ADMINISTRATIVE ASSISTANTS

Instead of hiring outside professionals to handle lower-level publishing chores, many companies are now having their administrative staff use DTP to take care of day-to-day publishing needs. Typically an administrative assistant might use DTP to prepare announcements, compile an informal in-house newsletter, or prepare in-house forms and documentation. She or he might prepare a proposal or report that contains graphs, tables, or charts generated from a data base, spreadsheet, or presentation software.

Depending on the firm, this procedure might range from using the advanced features of word processing software to using page layout and graphics presentation packages. At a large firm, a computer services department representative might set up a format or template that the office support staff might utilize. The administrative assistant might not necessarily be involved in the creation of the format or design for a particular project, but will instead work within the guidelines that others have created.

As software has become more powerful and easier to use, more and more of the publishing functions that were once taken care of by professionals are now being carried out by office support staff. This trend is certain to continue, and anyone interested in getting involved with business publishing should see a position as an administrative assistant as a step toward a position that might integrate higher-level DTP skills.

Administrative assistants who carry out DTP tasks needn't necessarily have comprehensive training in either graphic arts or DTP, but they should have basic computer and keyboarding skills. As with any other DTP-related job, diversity and flexibility are important characteristics. It is wise to be familiar with as many different current software and hardware applications as possible. Good language, writing, and communication skills are also helpful.

Salaries for administrative positions that involve DTP vary widely by region and company. Nevertheless, DTP skills will increase the likelihood of attaining positions with higher salaries and increased responsibility.

CORPORATE COMMUNICATIONS SPECIALISTS

Many of the DTP opportunities that you are likely to discover are in the business publishing sector and involve corporate communications. If you're involved in DTP at this level, you might be producing an annual report, a marketing brochure, an in-house newsletter, or a company policy booklet. Corporate communications is also likely to involve more than just page layout, design, or graphics skills. This is a particularly good area for those who are interested in combining writing and editing with their DTP skills. Corporate communications work that involves DTP commonly deals with the areas of marketing, advertising, and public relations. Let's examine this work more closely through the work of a computer graphics specialist who works for a large consulting company.

Profile: Margie Smith

Like many of her peers, computer graphics specialist Margie Smith entered desktop publishing through the back door. With no formal training—or awareness that she had the skills, talents, and instincts to create, manipulate, and fine-tune complex and sophisticated computer graphics and page layouts—she was given the task of supporting a computer consulting company's multimillion-dollar proposals.

As it turned out, it was the right job for the right person. Soon enough Smith learned the ins and outs of creating highly refined proposals, and she became an integral part of her company's consulting staff.

Smith's DTP work is an extremely important part of her company's work because she prepares the materials that sell her company's computer consulting services to potential clients. One of the most important aspects of her work is translating the raw ideas that are generated by the consulting team into final presentations.

"I usually am given the handwritten notes from the firm's consultants and am responsible for developing the layout for the final proposal," she says. "In order to accomplish that, I work with a staff of word processors who key in the text. I then copyedit and proofread their work, work on the design and format, and manage the project until it's ready to be delivered to our clients."

Though she primarily works on proposals, Smith also contributes her expertise by assisting in the development of marketing materials. She puts her graphics skills to work creating slide presentations and other support materials, using DTP tools for drawing and business presentations, such as Harvard Graphics and Lotus's Freelance.

Though the bulk of her work involves working with ideas and concepts that her firm's consultants have generated, she doesn't solely carry out the dirty work of others. "I often sit in on meetings and listen to ideas that are bounced around," she explains. "I assist the staff by creating computerized mock-up versions so that the staff could have a better visual idea of what we were working with. I sometimes go on-site with the consulting staff to help sell the ideas and add my input as part of the overall team."

Is Smith's position creative? It depends on the job, and sometimes she does have a lot of flexibility and freedom. "Sometimes the proposals are very cut-and-dried and there is not much room for creative presentation. With proposals sometimes people have done these kinds of things in a certain way for a long time and they don't want to change something that's worked for them in the past," she says. "In other situations we really bounce ideas around, like one proposal for a large banking firm we designed around a format that was similar to *Crain's Chicago Business* to create a proposal for a large bank. We bought a color printer for that and it was a really sharp proposal."

Through her work on proposals, Smith has branched off into specializing in other DTP areas. "Computer graphics has become my specialty. I've become adept at creating logos, scanning logos and touching them up, designing charts and graphics that translate information into pictures and images," she says. This is an area that she plans to pursue further in the future.

Her job has allowed for a lot of growth and learning. "I fell into this," she says. "The company needed me to learn Lotus Freelance, and from there I went and tried out a lot of different packages and ultimately became the company's in-house specialist."

Smith has no formal training, but she credits her work at a previous company with developing her eye for design and presentation. The technical expertise she gained on her own. "At a previous job I worked around a lot of designers and artists, and that type of environment rubbed off on me," says Smith.

Smith considers the collaborative work she does with others to be the best part of the job. "I love the collaboration," she says. "For me there's nothing better than having the chance to work on ideas as part of a team. Sharing and brainstorming ideas is fun, and to have the ability to express my creativity, which I did not know that I had, within a productive work environment, you can't beat that."

Smith has great enthusiasm for those entering the field but cautions students to learn as much as they can about the field before they try to jump into the work environment. "On a basic level you have to learn as many different software packages as you can and to keep your eye on the what's happening, what's changing, and what's coming up around the corner," says Smith.

One area in which she expects to see a lot of opportunity is multimedia. Already she sees this area coming into play in her everyday work. "In the next few years we're going to see more and more video integration with DTP," Smith explains. "Computer graphics specialists will be putting pieces of videotape into a document on a diskette." Smith sees multimedia development unfolding in the medical field, in the sciences, and in marketing. "We're going to be seeing a lot of self-running presentations, as opposed to paper presentations. These new tools will combine animation and straight text, and companies are going to need people who are capable of combining many different mediums," she notes.

For those breaking into the field, Smith suggests becoming involved with professional organizations like those listed in Appendix B. "Students shouldn't be afraid even to just pop into a meeting. You get to network with others and see what's really happening in the business world—things you can't learn from a textbook," she says.

Smith advises students who want to crack into the DTP field to put a quality portfolio together. "Samples are so important," she says. "And the key thing for me when I look to hire someone is that the samples should somehow be different, unusual, and unique."

When hiring, Smith also looks for other qualities. "I look for somebody who has more training than I, who works well in a team of workers, especially if they were going to be working on projects like proposals. Good communications skills are very important. The person has to be able to speak up when they need to, yet should know how to be a good listener. I also look for people who are really interested in the field, someone who really enjoys what they are doing and has a commitment to the field," she says.

According to Smith, the employment outlook in corporate communications appears good over the next few years. While today's salaries are not exceptionally high, they are beginning to increase. Computer graphics specialists in a corporate environment can expect to start in the $20,000 to $30,000 range.

TECHNICAL WRITERS

Technical writing is one of the largest areas of growth for work that incorporates a DTP component. Since the coming of the machine age in the 19th century there has been a consistent need for instructions—the more sophisticated the machinery, the more complex and detailed the set of instructions that are necessary. The more technology that became available, the more companies needed to communicate about it.

What do technical writers do? On a basic level, technical writers are the people who put together instructions that inform individuals about how to either use a product or complete a task. It is the technical writer's job to effectively communicate the work that the engineers, mechanics, and instructional designers have created.

As our society has grown more and more technologically oriented, the need for technical communicators has increased rapidly. Look around your house. Consider the volume of documentation that abounds. There are owner manuals for everything from the VCR, to the food processor, to the Nintendo machine, and that's not even considering the personal computer that might occupy your desk.

In industry and business the volume of this type of documentation increases severalfold. Robotic production equipment, computerized heating and air conditioning controls, digital voice mail—all of these require clear, concise documentation that explains in detail the device's features, how to use them, remedies for problems, and unique operating situations. This may be true whether the company is "high-tech" or not.

But where does DTP fit in? Today's technical writers are required to be able to produce a finished product. They must be able to communicate technical information to an often "untechnical" audience, and they must be able to put it in a form that amplifies the message and that can be reproduced quickly and cheaply.

From the time that electronic publishing was introduced, technical writing and DTP were a perfect marriage. With the coming of DTP technology, companies acquired the ability to efficiently produce camera-ready users manuals and instructional documentation. They could continually update their written work to match the changes in their products. By bringing the production of these materials in-house, a company could easily alter its publications without having to start from scratch, and it could respond to the increasing demands of a technologically hungry customer base.

With that in mind, here are profiles of two different technical communicators who utilize DTP as an integral part of their job. Maureen McGurn and Doug Feigin both work for Landis & Gyr Powers, an international company that specializes in building controls. One of the main foci of their business is the manufacturing and maintenance of computerized air-conditioning and heating control systems for buildings. Both work as part of the company's technical communications department.

Profile: Maureen McGurn

Maureen McGurn went to work as a technical writer at Landis & Gyr in 1986. Although in the past technical writers were not required to produce the actual documentation—they just wrote the materials and someone else put it into final form—McGurn has always been in the dual role of desktop publisher and writer. Typically McGurn works on installation instructions, technical manuals for in-house staff and field personnel, customer documentation (owners manuals) to tell the customers about the product and how to use it, and software documentation.

McGurn sometimes writes from scratch, but often she works closely with the company's engineers, who give her either their notes to work from or sometimes their rough first drafts. Often she receives this material in electronic form via a modem or on disk. She then transfers the information into her own computer system. She can then edit and lay out the material right at her own workstation.

For some technical writers the DTP element is minimal. Once "the look" of a document is created, they go about their writing by plugging their work into an already established form. They are not integrally involved in the actual design of how the documentation will look in final form. This is not the case for someone like McGurn. While she does not create a new format for every piece of work she puts together, she is an important part of the team that develops the formats for new types of documents that Landis & Gyr never did before.

Though she works with materials that are highly technical and intricate, McGurn considers her work to be very creative. "I'm a writer, and that assumes a certain level of creativity," she says. "We create everything—the manuals, the text, the look that we want something to have. A lot of our work is conceptualizing how to transmit the information to the user in the most effective way. It also involves making something that is pretty cut-and-dried accessible, and to take very technical information and make it readable and understandable."

Like many of her contemporaries, McGurn didn't start out to become a technical writer. Until recently schools did not offer much in the way of programs for technical communicators. She was originally a science teacher and then worked as textbook editor. She was looking for a way to combine her interests and decided to go back to school to learn about technical communications. "I do have some formal training, but as in many other professions, a lot of it has been on-the-job," she says. As for the desktop publishing skills, all of that was learned after she came to work for Landis & Gyr.

McGurn likes the integration of her job. She is with a project from the beginning and sees it through to its final form, and she says she loves working with computer tools: "I like working on a system; it's a lot easier for me to write and edit and put ideas together on the computer. DTP automates a lot of the elements that I would hate to do if I had to do them by hand. I like having the control that DTP gives me. I like the formatting, making the pages look nice. It's kind of fun to do that stuff, not working with just straight text."

McGurn works in conjunction with the department's technical illustrators, incorporating the computer-generated drawings into her documents. "I like that part of the work, placing and sizing the drawings so that they work well with the rest of the documentation," she says.

Like many others who rely on DTP technology to perform their jobs, McGurn notes that the only problems she finds with her work are connected to inadequacies of the hardware and software: "Sometimes the systems just don't do what we want them to do, and that can be very frustrating, and sometimes the systems just fail. We work under very tight deadlines and if you have a hardware failure, or you lose information or you can't get at it, for whatever reason, you're in big trouble."

According to McGurn, technical writing and communication is going through a growth period and there are lots of opportunities for people in the field. Not only are all kinds of new technologies becoming available that require support by technical writers, but the tools and media that are available for technical writers are opening up all kinds of opportunities that never existed before. "If we are truly going to go toward on-line documentation, that's not just a question of taking a manual and putting it on-line. That would be the wrong way to approach it," she says. "The right way is to have an understanding of how the user will access the information, what kind of information they will need to have and how they will go about using that information. The opportunity will be in areas that look at how the person interacts with the system." Whole new areas of study and work are developing that will incorporate these factors. You may want to check with your guidance counselor or your school's career center about areas like human factor engineering that look at how people use and process information.

For the student who wants to become a technical writer, McGurn suggests concentrating on developing strong writing skills. "If your school offers classes in technical writing, by all means take it," she says. According to McGurn, it is important to learn about the ways that people learn and process information through coursework in psychology, educational psychology, and instructional design. "It's also a good idea to get some technical training. If you're going to be a technical writer, you're only going to be better at it if you have a basic understanding of what an engineer does, or what a chemist does," McGurn adds.

As for the graphic and presentation aspects of what she does, McGurn suggests taking a two-dimensional design class, a typography class, and some type of desktop publishing layout and design class. In her opinion, versatility will separate you from the next person in landing a job.

McGurn says she thinks that technical writers earn good salaries. Entry-level technical writers with a four-year degree and no experience could expect to start at approximately $25,000 a year in 1992, with $50,000 to 60,000 being at the upper end of the scale.

Often companies like Landis & Gyr will hire individuals on a contract basis, especially for the layout and design of larger projects. "This is a good way to become involved if you are considering coming into the field," McGurn suggests. "We look for people with strong desktop publishing skills—someone who would be able to learn our system very quickly. On the other hand, some jobs will require more of a written emphasis and the DTP skills are less important. We look for people who have strong writing skills. You can train people to use the DTP system, but it is much more difficult to train people to do the writing."

McGurn sees a lot of changes and innovations on the horizon. "We do almost everything on paper right now," she says. "What is going to change in a big way is that more and more of our work will be delivered to our customers electronically. Some of that will be built into the products on-screen, some of what will go out on-line so that customers can get up-to-date publications on their own computers. It still will require desktop publishing skills— we'll still be creating pages and layouts, but the form that the final product will take will be a computer monitor instead of a piece of paper." Users are looking forward to this "paperless publishing" because they won't have to be lugging huge volumes to their job sites.

Profile: Doug Feigin

Doug Feigin is employed as a technical illustrator, a job that he loves but never expected to have. Feigin uses computerized design tools to develop drawings for the documents that technical writers like Maureen McGurn produce. Like McGurn, Feigin works closely with the engineers to enhance Landis & Gyr's technical documentation. It is Feigin's job to visually enhance the written documentation so that customers and field personnel have an accurate and clear picture of how Landis & Gyr's products work.

Feigin has been with Landis & Gyr since 1990, and prior to his joining the company's technical communications department, he had never worked in a DTP capacity. In fact, he never had done any computerized artwork and had only done technical illustration for a short time.

"Everything I did before I began working here was pen-and-ink. When I came to this company, they had this computer software and I was afraid to step up to it. On the interview, my co-worker showed me how easy it was to draw on this thing, and the timesaving over working with pen. It didn't take any time at all. I was up and running within a week," he says. Feigin is surprised what computers have done for artists. "Growing up I was very anti-computer. I didn't see it as a tool. All of a sudden this stuff is here, and it's wild the stuff that you can do."

Doug landed at Landis & Gyr because he had some important skills and interests that the company knew it could put to good use. "I liked art and I liked mechanical things," he says. Feigin studied fine art in school but never imagined that he would put it together with his mechanical interests. After college he had an opportunity to combine some of those skills as an illustrator. But it was his other love and interest that completed his credentials for being a technical communicator. Since he was a child, Doug has loved to tinker with mechanical objects, especially cars. He was the kind of person who liked to take things apart and put them back together just to see how they worked. Landis & Gyr gave him the opportunity to combine his two strongest interests together in a unique and powerful way.

"All my life I've been into art, which gives me an advantage over people who have just been into engineering and drafting, which is the areas that you see most technical communicators coming from," he says.

Though we don't often think of the art and technical worlds coming together, Doug Feigin says that his training and skill as an artist make him bring his illustrations to life so that he is really able to communicate to the users of Landis & Gyr equipment. "I have the ability to see the ways that shadows fall on a part, even if I don't have the light that way. I can show depth and dimension. And it's those extra elements that make our customers, clients, and field personnel understand how to use our equipment."

Landis & Gyr uses an integrated set of software to desktop-publish its documentation. This sophisticated set-up ties together layout and design, typesetting, editing, writing, and illustration. Feigin's workstation is electronically connected with McGurn's so that the drawings he produces can be placed alongside the written work that others have prepared.

Some of the things that Feigin illustrates include: exploded views of parts (that show all the different parts that make up a product), assembly views (that show how to install a product), technical instructions, and cover art.

Because of the new tools that DTP has provided the artist, Feigin produces his drawings in ways that are very different from those of the traditional illustrator. Although he sometimes draws something from sight, in the way that traditional illustrators have always worked, he tries to not create his images from scratch. Often he takes a photograph of the object and scans it into his computer system. The scanning process converts the photographic image into a digital computer format that will allow him to enhance and manipulate it. Sometimes he takes someone else's rough sketch or less-detailed version of the illustration and scans it into his computer system.

Feigin is an integral member of the Landis & Gyr technical communication process. In order to make his work be as meaningful and useful as possible, he takes extra effort to work with the company's engineers and writers. "I like to go back to the source and be sure that I'm going to be able to communicate what they want me to communicate," he says.

Feigin feels that his position is a very creative one. "It's not like drafting, where you have a lot of straight lines. You have to be able to show a part in a way that is natural, so that it's not just a print of a part. You have to be able to show a three-dimensional part and convey what it is, instead of a blueprint, and you have to show it in a way that the engineers and writers want the customer to see," he says.

The computerization of technical illustration has changed and improved the job, allowing artists like Doug Feigin to work efficiently and productively in a way that they were unable to do in the past. "One of the most significant things is that traditionally if you had to draw several drawings that were similar, you'd have to draw the first one separately and then trace it in ink again, again, and again, making the minor changes. Here you can copy the drawing with the click of a switch, instead of having to redraw the whole thing. You don't have to reinvent the wheel. You don't go home with ink in your pores," he says.

Feigin foresees that there will be lots of jobs available for technical illustrators. Though the documentation may take on new forms, the technical illustrator's role in the technical communication process will always be there, and there will be new and exciting computer tools for artists to communicate with.

Feigin advises future technical illustrators to be as well rounded as possible, whether their background is in drafting or engineering or in the fine arts. "If they are approaching it from drafting or engineering, they should move more toward fine arts to get a better handle on how to communicate to real people. Most of your audience will not be engineers," he says. "You need the mix. Likewise, if you're approaching it strictly from the fine arts side, if you don't have a technical background you won't be able to communicate the basics."

For the student interested in technical communication, coursework should include illustration and graphic design plus drafting, three-dimensional design, and basic core science classes like physics and geometry.

Students can expect starting salary ranges in the mid-$20,000 if they have an associate or bachelor's degree. With experience in the field, they can make as much as $55,000 to $60,000.

When asked what he would look for in an entry-level technical illustrator, Feigin was quick to answer. "Do they know how to draw? It doesn't matter if they can use the computer, because at this point it is so easy. If they can do it in pen-and-ink on board and can communicate in pen-and-ink, it's nothing to just sit someone down and show them how to do it on a computer. If they can draw and have the computer skills, that's just an added bonus."

DIRECTORY PUBLISHERS

Directory publishing is one of the specialties that has emerged from the DTP revolution. Because computer-based publishing has an infinite capacity to continually keep information up-to-date, DTP has allowed companies, associations, organizations, and publishers to get involved in publication of directories of every imaginable kind. Organizations can now share current information about their membership on a regular basis while keeping their costs to a minimum. From Vision Link Educational Foundation's *Who Is Who in Service to the Earth* to the National Society of Performance and Instruction's membership directory, DTP is an important tool in the exchange of information about people, products, and services.

Directory publishing typically brings together computer tools like data bases and page layout software to allow an organization to output fully typeset pages that are sorted and organized by a variety of categories. The most common examples of directory publishing would be your town's version of the yellow pages. But there are countless variations on this theme. Spend an afternoon in your library's reference section and you'll find an amazing assortment of directories that categorize and arrange people, businesses, and their products. If you like what DTP has to offer, enjoy the logic of computer programming, and have a knack for organizing, sorting, and manipulating data, directory publishing is an area that you should explore. In the next section we'll look at a directory publisher that uses DTP.

Profile: City Spirit Publications

Jerome Rubin started City Spirit Publications in 1986. He was short on practical knowledge about the publishing business, but long on inspiration and dedication. Rubin had an idea for a guide or directory series and the will to figure out the details along the way. He started the business out of his small Brooklyn apartment and soon began to sell his ideas to the advertisers that would eventually support his publications, an unofficial yellow pages for health, wellness, and the environment that would come to be known as *New York Naturally, New Jersey Naturally,* and *Connecticut Naturally.*

Though he imagined that computers would eventually come into play in the support of his small, growing business, he imagined that the books would be assembled through conventional means. The first edition he published was traditionally typeset and assembled. He employed a graphic designer, pasteup artist, and typesetting service for the first *New York Naturally.* The results were clean and professional.

As his business began to become more established, it became clear that City Spirit would be publishing books on a regular basis. Rubin needed a reliable means of automating the production of information that regularly recurred, which sent him in search of a computer solution. He had several important needs. He needed a way to produce his directories cheaply and efficiently. He also needed a way to easily update, modify, and change the information that appeared in his directories.

City Spirit was a perfect candidate for desktop publishing. As soon as he was able, Rubin invested in a computer, a laser printer, and some desktop publishing software. "It's funny to look back at the beginnings of how we got into desktop publishing," he says. "It was exciting, but also very nerve-racking because I had to learn all about how the stuff works and still keep the rest of the business going."

The second *New York Naturally* partially utilized the computers, but many of the book elements were still traditionally generated. "If I were to do it all over again, I would have invested more time and money in learning the software and hardware. That would have saved us a lot of time and we could have gotten fully computerized sooner," he says. "Fortunately the software and hardware has gotten more user-friendly, but still it's so powerful, and in the beginning we just didn't know how to use all the features that were packed into it."

By the third edition, the *Naturally* series had expanded to three states and moved to full computerized production. One of the main improvements was a shift to storing the directory information in a data base that allowed quick updating of information and the ability to intermingle old information with new. This also shortened the amount of time it would take to produce each directory so that he could extend the period of time for advertisers to come into the book. "Now that we generate the directory using data-base publishing we can turn around the book in a few days, instead of a few weeks. It allows us to make changes up until the very last minute, and in the publishing business that's very important."

Rubin employs several people in desktop publishing capacity. Like many other small publishers, he uses free-lance desktop publishers and contracts with different people for different specialties. "Using free-lancers allows me to get specialized service so that each job gets done by someone who knows how to do that job well," he says.

Rubin employs a free-lance desktop publisher who creates advertisements for the guidebooks. "We work with our customers to create the advertising ideas, and we'll create rough sketches of the ads and send them along to Sam, who refines them and sends us back proofs. We'll then fine tune them and send them to our clients for approval," he explains. Rubin relies on Sam Moore to turn the advertisements around quickly and to be sensitive to the clients' requests. Moore gets paid per advertisement and, depending on the complexity of the work, earns $30 to $40 an hour for his services.

City Spirit also uses the services of a company that specializes in color separation and the generation of cover artwork. "Those people are desktop publishers, too, but the difference is that they've invested in some very expensive equipment. It's still too expensive for a business like ours to handle that stuff in-house," says Rubin. "Color DTP work will eventually be the standard and in the next few years the equipment will get cheaper and easier to use. Right now I know that I can get somebody to take care of that fairly inexpensively."

Finally in regard to DTP, Rubin uses his editorial staff to handle the most important part of the production of his books. One of the editors handles the directory and guidebook sections. He not only edits the articles and features, but also handles the layout at the same time, all computerized. "It's funny, I would have never imagined when we started this that I'd have someone who was working on editorial and administrative functions also handle the layout work, but the technology has allowed many jobs to be consolidated. It's perhaps more difficult on the staff people because they're expected to handle a lot of different aspects of a job, but from a publisher's perspective it enables us to cost-effectively put out a quality product," he says. Rubin explained that the editor makes in the $25,000 to 30,000-a-year range.

When employing individuals who work on desktop publishing tasks, City Spirit has some important criteria. "Formal training is not that important to us, nor does the individual have to have a specialized degree, although it doesn't hurt," says Rubin. "I look for flexibility and the ability to handle several different tasks at the same time. The small publishing business requires people to be able to work under pressure and to shift priorities, often at a moment's notice." Rubin also explains that no matter how well planned his production schedule is, work tends to come in spurts, with a heavy workload always coming around deadline time.

"As far as the computer applications go, it is not essential that anyone know any particular software package. Versatility is more important—the more and different stuff that someone knows, the better. Whether they learn that on their own, or formally, is not important," he says. "I think it's more important that the individual understands conceptually what the software and hardware should be doing. Our work is specialized and unique to us, and it's important for someone to understand the bigger picture. The best people that have worked for us have been able to be patient and work through the inevitable problems that computers serve on them. So problem-solving skills are very important."

Rubin sees a lot more individuals like himself who have been able to find a specialized area in which to publish. Desktop publishing has enabled him to put out the same kinds of quality materials that larger businesses are putting out. "DTP has created many opportunities for small business people like myself, which in turn creates opportunities for many of the people who might be reading your book. For students who are starting out, small publishers provide an important training ground and an opportunity to really learn all the different sides of a business," he explains.

GOVERNMENT AGENCIES

The largest business publishers in the United States and Canada are governmental agencies. Your local municipality, along with the agencies that make up your state and federal government, all combine to produce a startling amount of printed materials. They produce documentation and texts of every kind, from contracts and proposals, to booklets and manuals, to forms and applications.

In much the same way that private businesses have begun to embrace the cost advantages and efficiency of desktop publishing, so too has the government. As a result, DTP opportunities in government agencies will grow severalfold over the next few years. For beginning DTPers, this is an excellent area to hone your skills.

Those with DTP skills can expect to find opportunities at every level of government, in many of the same roles we've outlined for private business publishers. Government agencies utilize technical writers and illustrators. They compile and produce reports, proposals, and directories. Agencies use DTP for writing and editing, typesetting, page layout and design, image manipulation, illustration, and more.

If you are interested in working in a DTP capacity for a government agency, start by taking a trip to your local or school library and read through some recent issues of *Federal Jobs Digest*. This bimonthly publication lists federal job opportunities. Look for the special issue *Introduction to the Federal Employment Process* for tips on landing a job with Uncle Sam. Another publication that would be helpful in this process is *Federal Career Opportunities,* a biweekly magazine that also lists federal job openings.

For information on careers on the local, state, and federal level, consult Daniel Lauber's *The Complete Guide to Finding Jobs in Government* (© 1989 Planning Communication, River Forest, IL). Your reference librarian and school guidance counselor will have additional information on government opportunities.

CHAPTER 5

GRAPHIC ARTS

The world of graphic arts is changing very quickly. In the early 1980s, if you were to visit with a designer or artist, you'd likely see that person in front of a drafting table. Computers were considered to be cold and analytical and not the kind of tools that artists were likely to be comfortable with. Indeed, there was much discomfort when computers began to show up in art departments and design studios.

Desktop publishing has changed all that. Visit the same art departments of design studios today and you're likely to find computers with large-screen monitors, laser printers, and scanners.

Simply put, in the past decade computers and graphics software have become part of the graphic artist's tool box. And the same artists and designers who were at first resistant to these electronic tools are developing all kinds of new and innovative uses for them. In this section we will look at the ways that designers and graphic artists are working with DTP.

DESIGNERS

Designers are the very heart and soul of the graphic arts. It is their job to create and develop the concepts that make up the printed page. They are the creative part of the publishing process. Traditionally, designers would study a project and perhaps research appropriate photographs, illustrations, or other visual enhancements. They would pick out the appropriate type style and sizes. Then, perhaps using pen-and-ink or pencil, they might sketch their concepts. They would work along with a typesetter and printer to prepare a *comp* (comprehensive), or finalized version of the project.

The advent of DTP has not changed the role of the designer, though some of the process has changed. Our next profile looks at the work of designer Jim McGuire.

Profile: Jim McGuire

Jim McGuire's graphic design firm works in conjunction with advertising agencies, marketing firms, and businesses in the development of everything from corporate identity work like logos, letterheads, and capabilities brochures; to product or service brochures and newsletters; to annual reports and exhibit displays. McGuire is a traditionally trained graphic artist who incorporates both electronic tools and traditional design tools into his projects.

Like many other designers, McGuire works with a wide range of businesses and in a variety of roles. Some of his current clients include companies in the electronics business, business-to-business vendors, and a nonprofit historical society.

Like many designers and desktop publishers in general, McGuire's role is often a consulting one. "It is usually our job to help our clients develop concepts," he says. "Typically a client might come in with some rough idea or preexisting design, at least in terms of its marketing objectives. Then we take that information and either enhance it or build off it to create a finished product that suits that client."

As a designer, McGuire is very service oriented, and he must tailor his work to meet the needs of his client. "Every client is different. Sometimes we act strictly as designers and the client provides the copy, or sometimes we will do both, depending on their needs and capabilities," he says.

Has McGuire's work changed with the advent of DTP? He thinks so. The service itself hasn't changed that much, but the way he will go about his work has. "I still do design work traditionally and I do work on the computer. Today I have more choices than I had 10 years ago," he explains. "Designers now have a larger bag of tricks. By being able to do both, I can analyze a situation or project and make the decision about whether it's a good job to do on the computer or a good project to do traditionally," he says.

Though many would like to think otherwise, McGuire believes that good designers shouldn't rely heavily on either set of tools. "The important thing to realize is that the computer is not the end-all tool—at least not yet," he says.

McGuire has a bachelor's degree in design and recommends it as an important starting point for a career. "You can acquire the knowledge in other ways, but school will give you a good foundation. Designers need to know about the principles of space, principles of typography, the principles of art in general. You need to be sensitive to light and shade, to balance. You have to know what to look at, what makes something good, what makes something not good. At the very least a design program will introduce you to those things," he says.

As far as computer training goes, McGuire learned on his own. "I just jumped in," he explains. "I had real projects to work on. I used an audio tape series to help me learn Quark Xpress, Adobe Illustrator, and Adobe Photoshop."

According to McGuire, DTP has created a lot of competition in the design field. With the advent of lower-priced hardware and the expanded capabilities of DTP software, many individuals without training or experience, who might not otherwise be involved in design work, are offering design services to businesses and individuals. Many companies who had once used outside vendors in a design capacity have taken those needs in-house to save money and time.

"We've gotten into a situation where many people are doing DTP without any design background. They are creating pieces that are of lesser quality, forcing the standards to go down. Clients have also begun to say to themselves that it shouldn't cost that much to do. In the end, many of these people are buying mediocre design, and good design still has a premium to it," he says. "Still there are many clients that know the difference, and the individuals that have that balance between traditional design and computer skills will do well for themselves."

McGuire advises those interested in design careers to be well studied. "Learn and study as much as you can about the arts. It's important to be well-rounded," he says. "Learn as many software programs as you can, because the opportunities vary from one design firm to the next. Be familiar enough with the software to at least do some simple jobs with the software and know how to take good ideas through from concept to their finish."

As with all of the other opportunities in the DTP world, salary for design jobs varies widely. However, designers with solid traditional training and computer skills can expect to be well paid for their services, especially after they've gained some hands-on experience. Many people in the design field work in a free-lance capacity and as such they get paid an hourly wage. Beginning free-lance design-ers can expect to make in the $8 to $18-per-hour range. Full-time beginning designers can expect to make $16,000 to $23,000 a year, with additional fringe benefits.

When hiring designers, McGuire likes to see a clean, well-balanced portfolio. "I like to look at the way they've handled concepts, how they've gone about solving a prob-lem," he says. McGuire suggests including only your best work in a portfolio. He also recommends including not just finished work, but sketches that show an individual's process.

McGuire recommends that the beginning designer have perseverance. "You've got to keep knocking on doors all the time. Call back all the places that you've called on that have told you, 'No we don't have any openings at the moment,' " he says. "It's a numbers game, especially in the design field. It's a question of being at the right place at the right time. Don't be discouraged by the first three or four interviews that don't turn out successfully. Someone you called last week or last month might have just let someone go, or they might have a new client and need someone else to fill out their staff."

ADVERTISING REPRESENTATIVES

One of the business areas that has greatly benefited from the introduction of desktop publishing is the advertising field. The new technology has allowed advertising agencies to easily follow up on their creative instincts and give their clients a much greater range of choices to meet their advertising needs. It has also allowed many smaller companies to bring their advertising production work in-house, giving them greater flexibility and control over their work. In many ways DTP and advertising are a perfect marriage, and there is certain to be continued growth in this area.

Many of the larger advertising agencies have developed full-scale DTP departments that take the raw ideas that the creative staff and account executives generate and translate them into full-fledged advertising campaigns. Regardless of the size of the agency, advertising professionals at every level are likely to utilize computerized page layout and design, even as they generate rough drafts for their advertising campaigns. Designers like Jim McGuire, profiled in the last section, are likely to either work with, or be employed by, an advertising agency. Agencies are likely to use DTP personnel to provide everything from layout and typesetting, to illustration and image processing.

In the following section we profile Walter Goldstein, an account executive and partner of a smaller advertising agency. Increasingly, in his day-to-day work, Goldstein uses DTP to build and work up advertising ideas that he can share with his clients and his partner. Some of the work he prepares is camera-ready, but often he will work with a desktop publishing service, service bureau, or traditional typesetter to output his final versions of advertising materials.

Profile: Walter Goldstein

Walter Goldstein is a partner in a small advertising agency, Goldstein and Fromer, that handles the advertising and public relations needs of medium to large businesses. The agency's specialty is doing business-to-business advertising campaigns. Some current clients include a company that sells products to dentists, the industrial and athletic division of a large sports beverage manufacturer, an office supply manufacturer, a real estate company, and even a golf course.

Goldstein's agency uses DTP as a tool to help flesh out rough ideas. DTP has enabled it to give its clients a better sense of the finished product and to do so quickly and efficiently. Typically after meeting with a client, Goldstein will generate a sample advertisement or collateral piece. "We'll do the headlines, subheads, and the body copy, and perhaps scan in a photograph or illustration," he says.

Advertisers have to put out their message in a very efficient way, and DTP has allowed agencies to show their clients how subtle variations can have an impact on how the consumer perceives a product. Before DTP it was much more time-consuming to allow for the same range of choices: Creating a different version of a particular ad campaign could take several days or even weeks. Now the same process can take place almost instantaneously. "Perhaps the best enhancement that DTP has given us is that you can try out a lot of different ideas very quickly," says Goldstein.

DTP allows an agency like Goldstein and Fromer to produce high-quality professional materials, so that even though it is small in size, it is able to work with larger companies and give them personalized service. "The thing about smaller agencies like ours is that each of us here carries out many functions, and the DTP is just one of the many things that each of us does. There's less division here, and as we work with a client we'll move with the project from concept to actual artwork," Goldstein says.

Goldstein believes that the real opportunities for DTP in the advertising field will be for those who have a strong background in traditional design and who know how to use computerized page layout and graphic manipulation. "Often people get into advertising through learning DTP and they never learn the finer points of design," he says. "Be a designer first and a desktop publisher second. Start with the concepts and a creative feel for how to make things look good in an impactful way."

Goldstein suggests that students determine what kind of role they would like to play. If they want to be involved in the creative part of the advertising business, they should put their emphasis on design and becoming a good communicator. He suggests that the technical skills can come later.

"I tell people who want to get into the business to take every opportunity they get to work on design, and I'm not sure that schools are the place to get that training. You need to learn how to do it hands-on," he says. He encourages students to take every opportunity they can to try out their design skills, be it for a school production or a local organization. "Take products that you like and make up ad campaigns for them. Learn to be a decent writer. Learn to be a good communicator," he says.

Goldstein advises those interested in using DTP in advertising to be well rounded and balanced. "Ultimately advertising, marketing, and DTP are fields of communication, be it visual or with the word. I think it's important for someone who wants to get into the field to have a feel for how to say something in an impactful way, and to know how to integrate visual ideas and words," he says.

Salary ranges in the advertising field vary greatly depending on the size of the agency and the type of accounts they handle. Starting salaries for those who use DTP in the advertising field range from the low $20,000s to the low $30,000s. There is a lot of room for advancement for those who can integrate many skills.

BOOK PUBLISHERS

While desktop publishing has enabled the start-up of many small publishing businesses, mainstream book publishers have been slow to embrace this new means of production. As a business that has a long conservative history, book publishing has had a difficult transition into DTP. Many decision makers initially felt that they could not get the same quality that they achieved using traditional typesetting and production through the newer technology, and they were reluctant to change the procedures and techniques that they had been using successfully for so many years.

Still, like many of the other industries that we've profiled, the book publishing business is starting to shift much of its production to the desktop. The savings in time and money are too substantial for the companies to ignore; furthermore, the technology has improved so much that in many cases even the trained eye cannot distinguish between books that have been traditionally prepared and those that have been produced on desktop computers.

The shift by book publishers to DTP technology is likely to speed up throughout the rest of the 1990s. As a result there will be many job opportunities for people with DTP skills. The jobs will encompass every level of the book production process, from editors and writers, who will work with texts on-line; to book designers and illustrators, who will create the books' format and visual components; to typesetters and color separators, who will put the book into its more finalized form. There will be a trend toward the consolidation of jobs, so that individuals might be responsible for several aspects of the production process, but the need for trained DTP professionals will grow.

One way that mainstream book publishers are beginning to embrace DTP technology is through the use of editorial production companies that handle the editorial and production phases of a book project for the publisher. These companies are hired by a publisher to handle all the aspects of taking a book from an idea to the printed page. DTP has allowed them to become specialists in producing books efficiently and inexpensively.

The publishing company takes care of all the business elements of producing a book, including negotiating with an author, advertising, marketing, and distribution. This section will profile a manager at an editorial production house that specializes in elementary and high school textbooks.

Profile: Kathi Beste

Kathy Beste is the production director at Ligature, one such production house located in Chicago. Her company specializes in teaching and learning materials, textbooks, folders, workbooks, teacher's guides, and premium materials for textbook sales forces.

Ligature uses DTP exclusively, and it produces nearly all its materials in-house on Macintosh computers. The designers, typesetters, and editorial staff all work together and share information electronically. They deliver a nearly final product to a pre-press film house that handles the final preparation, outputting the electronic file received from Ligature to film, then delivering the finished film to a printer, who manufactures the actual book. (Chapter 6 discusses pre-press and service bureaus.)

As Ligature's production director, Beste must manage the intricacies of the textbook production process. She oversees the work of designers, typesetters, and artists and makes sure that the textbook arrives in the appropriate form at the film production house. Although her job entails a great deal of coordination, she considers it to be creative. "I'm not really involved in the design phase of each project, but I am in charge of figuring out how to get it produced, which requires me to come up with creative solutions," she says.

Beste has learned all of her skills on the job, including much of her computer expertise. Over the years she has developed an intricate knowledge of design, typesetting, and pre-press film production, as well as paper, printing, and binding. She regularly augments her skills, especially in computer applications, with training that she receives at seminars and trade shows.

While a lot of Beste's day-to-day work does not involve page layout and design—the kinds of activities that we normally associate with DTP—as a production director she has to keep abreast of all the new technology so that she can train staff and manage the work of others. Often she must act in a troubleshooting capacity and help other members of her production team to bring a project to its completion. "As we move forward into DTP, we have to keep the old, and add the new to it," she says, emphasizing the important balance that is necessary in her industry. "The problem is that most people only learn half the story, and end up having big problems in the middle of the production cycle. Then they want me to fix it, yesterday."

Beste believes that although DTP has added many twists to her job, the final product—the textbook—has not changed much at all. "Textbooks are still the same as they've always been. The market is very conservative and can't afford to be experimental. But how we create the final product has changed drastically," she says. "DTP has made it possible for me to do what in the past had been done by three or four people."

According to Beste, DTP in the book publishing field is a competitive field, but there are many opportunities for those who are good learners and willing to work hard. "If someone can buckle down and learn from special classes, seminars, and manuals, the possibilities are limitless," she says. She encourages students to learn as much as they can about computer software but says that the people who will really get ahead as desktop publishers in the book publishing business will have a comprehensive understanding of all aspects of publishing, including editing and printing. "The camera/production knowledge is essential if you want to be able to move up; it will help you become invaluable," she says.

As a production director, Beste echoes the advice of many of the other individuals we have profiled thus far. "Be humble and willing to learn as much as you can on the job," she says. She notes that book production is difficult and tedious work and it is likely to be very different than the kind of work one does in school. "Most of your first on-the-job assignments will not bear any resemblance to school assignments, and the deadlines will be much tighter. You will have to do many projects at once over a period of days or weeks, instead of just one due at the end of the semester." She suggests joining a local branch of one of the trade associations that often have one-day seminars to help you keep up with current trends and make connections.

New DTP hires in the book publishing industry can expect to start at a salary of between $12,000 and $17,000 a year for a full-time position with benefits. While that may seem low, there is substantial room for advancement, with the possibility of making as much as $40,000 to $100,000 a year as a production director. Many people start out working as free-lancers, earning an hourly wage of $8 to $15 per hour.

When looking for new staffers to bring into her production team, Beste looks for individuals who are willing to learn, have an ability to handle multiple tasks, and are organized and able to keep detailed track of things like artwork or photos, page logs, and job progress. She considers knowledge of software and hardware important but also notes that one needn't be an expert to land a job.

Similarly, she considers knowledge of type specifications and basic graphics to be important but emphasizes that much of that can be learned on the job. She looks for well-rounded candidates who have good communication skills, with a good command of the English language. She also likes to hire individuals who have working knowledge of a second language, especially Spanish.

Book production can be very stressful, and Beste suggests that the most successful workers are even-tempered and have interests beyond their work: "It's important for staff to have other outside interests besides work and DTP. This gives them a better perspective on things and tends to weed out people who create problems in crunch production time."

MAGAZINE PUBLISHERS

Desktop publishing has entered the magazine publishing field in a big way. By 1992 even some of the more traditional magazines, like *The New Yorker,* had switched over to desktop production. One article noted that the switch to DTP had saved *The New Yorker* publishing company, Advance Magazine Publishers, $1 million a year. *The New Yorker* was reluctant at first to use DTP tools, as it had such a classic look and longstanding tradition. The magazine's production department, however, has been able to accurately replicate the classic feel and look of the original typesetting specifications and allowed *The New Yorker* to produce the magazine effectively using modern tools and techniques.

While *The New Yorker* exemplifies a magazine that was able to successfully shift to DTP, the arrival of DTP has also brought about a whole new crop of magazines that were designed from the ground up with DTP in mind. Since about 1987 there has been an explosion of such magazines, both in the consumer and trade sectors. While a sluggish economy has slowed some of this growth, there are considerable opportunities for desktop publishers in the magazine publishing field. The next section describes the DTP components at a large monthly regional magazine.

Profile: Kerig Pope

Kerig Pope has worked in many capacities in the magazine publishing business, from intern to art director. As art director, Pope helped his employer, a well-established magazine, make the transition to DTP. Currently he serves as graphics systems manager, a position that oversees all the DTP components of his magazine's production.

Pope is in charge of making his magazine's DTP systems work. He works closely with the production director, trains staff members in DTP, and serves as in-house computer troubleshooter. Additionally he manages and translates all the electronic files that his magazine sends to a service bureau for final film output.

Magazine production, like book production, often involves many different people working on many different parts of the process. Articles get written by writers, who send their work along to editors, who in turn pass it along to typesetters and page layout staff. Similarly photographs and artwork are prepared by other individuals and then passed along to the production staff to be incorporated into the completed magazine. The roles at a magazine that uses desktop publishing are similar to those that were used prior to the introduction of DTP systems, but now the information is shared electronically.

This new dependence on computerized information has created the need for positions like graphics systems manager to make sure that computer information flows between departments efficiently, smoothly, and uniformly. It is a critical and demanding position, and an area that will demand capable individuals in the future. As DTP flourishes in the magazine world, it will become more complex and sophisticated, requiring individuals who are able to work well with electronic information, yet who are sensitive to the graphic and editorial aspects of the field.

Kerig Pope's job is multifaceted, and typical of the new kinds of positions that DTP is creating. "I do a lot of standard production work in terms of trafficking, keeping logs of what comes in and what goes out, but I'm also the staff person who answers all the questions. For instance, if someone wants to know how to create something, I'm the person they will call. I also make sure that everyone is trained in hardware and software," he says.

Pope started in the magazine business as an intern, a route that he recommends highly to others. "There's really no better way to do it, and if the student or person new to the work force can figure out a way to do it, it will ensure them a future in the business," he says. Pope learned DTP through the trial-and-error of intensive on-the-job experience. His magazine was eager to bring desktop publishing into its production and looked to Pope to learn about it and teach the rest of the staff. Two years later, he has become the resident DTP expert and an indispensable liaison between the magazine and the printing process. "I have some training in Quark Xpress, but by the time I did that it was more review than anything else," he says. "The training is not always so important. It's more of a question of being able to learn and absorb information from a lot of different sources."

As for opportunities for DTP in the magazine field, Pope believes that there are many, especially for people who are able to work in many different capacities. "In the next few years there's going to be a need for more and more people like myself," he predicts.

According to Pope, many companies that buy DTP systems don't really understand the complexity that they are getting involved with. "The people who sell the systems make you believe that it's going to be a piece of cake, but that's never the case. You find that when you get more than a few of the systems in, it requires some type of person to put it all together," he says. Pope also sees more and more opportunity for people who deal with and electronically process the information generated by magazines at pre-press houses and service bureaus.

"My advice is for students not to gear themselves to just one part of the production process," says Pope. "It's important to know about what editors do, what art directors do, what pre-press people do. As I mentioned earlier, interning is the way to go, and the best situation would be to intern at several different places. I could see interning at a service bureau, perhaps in the editorial or design department of a magazine. It's important to understand how all the different people work together."

Salary for DTP specialists who work on a magazine staff varies widely, depending on the company, the nature of the position, and geography. Graphic systems managers like Kerig Pope can expect to make salaries upwards of $30,000 to $60,000. "Someone who has some school training and perhaps an internship can expect to break in at $30,000," says Pope.

In keeping an eye out for staffers to work as part of his electronic publishing team, Pope looks for people who have a comprehensive understanding of computer hardware and software. But while knowledge of DTP applications is an important part of the work, Pope feels that perhaps more important for someone who will be involved with graphic systems management is to understand the logic and internal workings of computer systems. "In these kinds of positions, you have to know the systems from the inside out because you're going to be called on to have that knowledge to come up with solutions to inevitable problems," he says. But systems knowledge is only part of the puzzle. Pope suggests that graphic systems people be knowledgeable about the entire production process, from idea to final product. "You never know at which stage you're going to be called in," he says.

DESKTOP PUBLISHING SERVICES

One of the revolutionary aspects of desktop publishing has been the proliferation of small independent publishing services. Since its introduction in the mid-1980s, DTP has promoted small active businesses that provide valuable services to their communities. These new DTP businesses are part of a larger information explosion, and they have allowed even the smallest organization or business to get its information to the public in a professional and uncompromising way.

While the supply of competent individuals to carry out the layout and design tasks has increased, the demand for these services has increased severalfold as well. Individuals want more control over their messages, images, and information, and even if they are not equipped to carry out these tasks themselves, they want to work closely with those who do.

Thus the advent of the desktop publishing service. These new businesses act as an intermediary between an individual and the printed publication. They work in many different capacities, but they are built around their ability to meet the needs of their customers. They provide their clients with a customized service and the ability to produce sophisticated print media at an affordable price.

To get a better look at what these businesses are about and to see the employment opportunities, let's visit a desktop publishing business.

Profile: Alan May

Alan May's Alphabetics Inc. is on the second floor of a quiet street just off one of the main shopping streets in the Chicago suburb of Evanston, Illinois. May's office suite is small, yet tidy, professional, and busy. The white shelves are lined with computer paraphernalia, scanners, and a laser printer.

On any given day you're likely to catch either him or his assistant busily at work at their respective Macintosh work stations, composing or dressing up everything from new product catalogs, to artwork for magazine advertisements, to children's activity books and textbooks, to business forms and brochures, to newsletters and resumes. And as he would say it, "There's a lot more than meets the eye."

Alphabetics advertises itself in the yellow pages as a "prepublisher." In that capacity, it takes an idea or concept that a client has generated and turns it into a form that can be reproduced by a printer. "On a typical day we might work with a graduating college senior who needs a design and typesetting help for his or her resume, or we might be helping a corporate client fine-tune a business form," he says.

Not only will Alphabetics work with companies or individuals who need full-service typesetting, the firm also works in a consulting capacity. "Many companies will come to us when their in-house staff runs into a snag," May says. "They may need us to finish a job that they can't complete because of deadline constraints, or they might need our technical expertise."

It is not unusual for a business that does its own desktop publishing to come to Alphabetics because it needs to fine-tune its work. May's staff may suggest improvements to the client's own design and presentation, and they might be called on to teach the client to carry out the improvements. "We're not just typesetters by any means," says May. "Often the critical aspect of what we provide is service. We help clients do what they can't do for themselves."

Unlike many of his peers, Alan May had been in the printing and publishing business prior to the introduction of DTP technology. Yet unlike many who were in the printing business, he was quick to embrace the new technology and the freedom that it provided. Because he knows so much about the demands and requirements of both desktop publishing and the printing business, he is often able to act as an important intermediary between his customers and the print shop that eventually produces the final copy.

"I maintain relationships with several printers, because my clients are very diverse and I haven't yet found the right print shop that can meet the demands of all my clients," May says. "What I do, rather than get in the middle, is make the contact for my client, establish the parameters of the job, and get a price quote for them. I then pass the client directly on to the printer."

Since there are many desktop publishing services, May wants his clients to have a reason to come back to him. "My work with printers is an extra service that I can provide my clients with that will make them come to me rather than go to someone else. And it has worked really well for me. When they have a question about typesetting or printing they'll come to me first, which means that I have a first go at the job," he says.

Has the nature of May's work changed since he's gotten into DTP? "It used to be that people who had printing and typesetting needs would think out their work way in advance because it was very expensive to do typesetting work, and because of the price they'd be reluctant to make changes," he says. "Now they come in and say, I don't know what I want. Try these four versions and we'll see which one I like best."

Publishing and printing have always been businesses with tight deadlines, but for desktop publishing services, timely production is crucial to getting repeat business. "If we can't turn it around quickly, someone else is likely to be able to, and it's not something we can afford to chance," he says. Still, speed is not the only criterion for May's customers. May points to the fact that businesses like his have become as much consulting services as anything else.

Businesses like Alphabetics have made DTP an integral player in the development of business communications. May points to a set of forms that he was preparing for a large insurance firm. The form that he was creating had been through 17 revisions. "There's no way that they ever would have done this in the past; it would have cost them too much money. Each change would have cost them hundreds of dollars, but they needed for us to help them go through all the revision steps till they found the appropriate format—and because of DTP, they were able to make all those changes and not pay an arm and a leg for them," he explains.

What's in the future for DTP services like Alphabetics? According to May, the future of DTP will include a lot of high-end work that uses four-color process. It's not work he's going to jump into very soon, primarily because of the outlay necessary for the proper equipment, but in time he believes that his customers will demand it from desktop publishing services. "A lot of prepublishers are gearing up for color and high-quality work, but I believe that a lot of the DTP work will remain in the medium-quality range," he says.

May believes that there are lots of opportunities for students interested in the field, especially for those willing to work for others. "Businesses like ours are always looking for savvy young people who are dependable and flexible," he says. But he sees perhaps more opportunity in businesses that are bringing their publishing work in-house: "DTP is alive and well at advertising agencies, or even businesses like video rental libraries, who are looking to bring their publishing work in-house. It's definitely a growth industry, but it's a question of going where the work is."

While difficult economic times have created a lot of work for desktop publishers, there's also a lot of competition. "Right now things are tight all over, and small businesses like desktop publishing services are facing fierce competition. The market's saturated, but if you're current with the right software packages, and you can handle the pressure and demands of working on deadlines, there's plenty of opportunity," says May.

As with many of his DTP peers, May encourages students to be well rounded. "In order to find work you should be competent in at least two of the major page layout programs, and for Macintosh that's going to be Quark and Pagemaker, and at least two of the drawing programs like

Freehand, Adobe Illustrator. The more that you know, the more salable you are, and that's always going to be the case," he says. "And of course some sort of design background." For May that needn't necessarily be formalized training. "It can be just the ability to know what looks good on a page," he says. "It could be someone with a print background, like keyline pasteup, to someone who's an artist who draws. The ability to look at a page and determine that it's too light on this side, too heavy on that."

May has formal training in the arts and graphic design through studies at the Art Institute of Chicago, and he by no means discourages formal training or studies. "If they offer something at the school you're attending, then by all means take it. Classes are a good idea, even just to help determine if a student is really interested in the field. It's an interesting field, just like anything else, but if you're going to get into it, and spend eight or nine hours a day with your face four inches from the monitor, you better make sure that it's something that you like to do," he says.

Depending on the shop that you work for, May says that an individual who gets into DTP as part of a service like his can expect to start at a salary that ranges from $17,000 to $30,000 a year. "There's a lot of work out there, more and more of it all the time. It's a question of marketing your skills and learning as much as you can along the way."

CHAPTER 6

PRE-PRESS AND SERVICE BUREAUS

Desktop publishing has brought about a new degree of specialization and a host of new types of jobs and services. Many of these are carried out by service bureaus or pre-press facilities. These businesses focus on preparing materials for full-scale reproduction and do not typically carry out the design or creation of publications. Their final product is usually film or a transparency that will be used by a printer.

Like the desktop publishing services examined in the last chapter, they are usually the intermediary between designers or business publishers and a printer. What distinguishes the service bureaus from the smaller desktop publishing services is their ability to provide a wider variety of services and their investment in state-of-the-art specialized hardware.

Companies that have invested large amounts of time, money, and personnel into bringing their print production needs in-house through DTP are still not necessarily capa-

ble of producing the kind of output necessary for sophisticated projects. Simple two-color or black-and-white manuals, flyers, and marketing materials might be handled by
in-house DTP, but anything requiring a higher resolution
output, color, or integration of sophisticated graphic elements is going to require the services of a pre-press facility.
It simply costs too much money for the average company to
afford the necessary equipment. Furthermore, it is a far
more difficult process than the average DTP is capable of
handling. A typical desktop publisher might have the capacity to create beautiful pages and graphics on its desktop
computer, but being able to print those pages is a whole
other story, especially if they involve color.

Service bureaus and pre-press facilities operate in many
capacities, from outputting materials that others have already prepared to formatting documents, graphics, and
photographic material, often with the use of color. They
provide companies that do their own DTP work with the
know-how and the equipment to translate their electronic
information into a printable format.

TRANSITION IN THE FIELD

DTP has brought about a major transition in the pre-press
field, and it is a field that will see much growth through the

mid-1990s. If you like detail, have a sensitive eye for color and composition, and work well with computer systems, this will be a good area for you.

Pre-press services until recently handled graphic materials only in traditional formats (camera-ready pages). With the rise of DTP, they have had to develop new departments that deal with the electronic information they are receiving from their clients. It has created a need for individuals who have background and training in traditional printing and graphics, and who understand computer hardware and software.

Working in a pre-press environment is likely to expose you to a wide variety of materials and publications and to put you in touch with the latest and most sophisticated DTP equipment available.

Profile: Bob Skutnick

Bob Skutnick is the electronics systems development manager of Liberty Engraving, a large pre-press facility with an active interest in desktop publishing. He manages a group of electronic publishing specialists who handle all the necessary aspects of translating electronic DTP information that they receive from their clients into film.

Liberty works with many different kinds of businesses, and the range continues to grow. "Our involvement with clients that do DTP has gotten very diverse. Two years ago when we first started up this division, we dealt a little with magazines, where now we deal with a much broader scope," he says. "Now we deal not only with magazine production, but book production. We do a lot of retail work like newspaper inserts and catalogs. We work with companies like Sears and Montgomery Ward. More and more of these companies are moving to DTP for production and need companies like ours to help them put together a finished product."

Liberty runs a 24-hour electronic bulletin board which allows a client to send in DTP files over phone lines. Some clients deliver their output to Liberty on computer disk. Whatever the format, the electronic publishing specialists then begin to make the necessary preparations for output.

For a magazine, that might mean scanning and touching up four-color photographs using high-resolution equipment, doing color separation (a complex and highly refined process), and eventually replacing the lower-resolution images the magazine production staff had put in place to indicate placement and position. In the case of color artwork and photographs, the electronic publishing specialists will do color correction and send proofs to their clients for approval. They will then carefully proof the pages to make sure that they are consistent and the colors are correct, and then bring all the information together on their film output equipment.

According to Skutnick, the ideal electronic publishing specialist is going to have a strong pre-press background with an in-depth knowledge of the particulars of traditional printing and graphic arts. "You could be a Macintosh guru, be learned in any one of a number of high-level DTP software packages, but that's only part of the story in pre-press," he says. "We've found that it's essential to have a knowledge of the printing business, traditional page make-up, typography, and keylining."

Students interested in electronic pre-press careers should have a basic familiarity with hardware and software. They should learn the major software packages, particularly on Macintosh computers. They should also get training in graphic arts production, be it from a school program or an apprenticeship or internship. Many of the pre-press skills can be acquired through traditional printing and graphic arts programs and through printing industry trade unions.

Electronic publishing specialists can expect to make between $30,000 and $50,000 a year, depending on their experience and the firm that they work for. Skutnick believes there will be an increased need over the next few years, especially in the areas of image processing and color separation.

QUICK PRINT SHOPS

One recent business trend that works hand-in-hand with DTP is the quick print shop. New advances in printing technology and an increased demand for profes-sionally printed materials have allowed the printing busi-ness to diversify. As a result, in the last decade quick print shops have become a regular part of the local busi-ness community.

These inexpensive, often franchised, printers allow even the smallest business access to professional printing at a fraction of the cost of standard print shops. Typically they provide a full range of medium-quality printing and copying services, with the promise of low cost and quick turnaround. Some of the best-known quick print chains are Sir Speedy, American Speedy, PIP, Minuteman, and Kinko's.

Although these print shops often work from the cam-era-ready originals that their customers provide, quick printers will typically use DTP for the typesetting and layout of jobs when their customers don't provide origi-nal artwork or copy. As such they will employ people with DTP skills as part of their in-house full-time staff or as free-lancers.

Quick print shops require DTPers who are able to work quickly on a wide variety of materials. Typically they might desktop-publish business cards, flyers, brochures, business forms, and stationery. Though salaries are likely to be lower than in other DTP areas, the quick print shop is an excellent training ground for those interested in DTP careers. It provides the opportunity not only to gain experience in computer skills, but also to receive a fundamental understanding of the way DTP and the printing process work together.

CHAPTER 7

FINDING A JOB

So you want to be a desktop publisher. You've read through the profiles in this book and you've decided that you're going to take a shot at getting involved in the field. This chapter will give you practical advice on how to zero in and land the job that you want.

Job hunting is a complex process, and there are many techniques and strategies that people like yourself can use to land a good job. You will find many excellent books on the subject in your local library and at your school's career center. Ask your guidance counselor or local librarian to make some recommendations.

Keep an open mind. Remember that 85 percent of all job opportunities are not publicized through conventional means like newspaper classified sections. Remember also that businesses look at employees as long-term investments. Many times experience and training are less important than your potential. Businesses are always on the lookout for solid, dependable people who are willing to work hard and learn, even if they don't have a lot of experience.

There are many ways to go job hunting. It will take time, and depending on the nature of the job market and the economy in your part of the country, you should prepare yourself for a long-term approach. This might mean taking on part-time work while you are job hunting, or joining a service like the temporary employment agency that we profile later in this chapter. Use your time effectively, and with perseverance (and a little luck) you'll land a good job. Learn how to market and present your skills and abilities and you will get the attention of the business for which you want to work.

Though the newspaper classified ad section is the first place that job searchers think to look for jobs or job listings, most career experts and experienced job searchers agree that concentrating your job hunt on classified listings is a risky and inefficient means of finding a good job. The likelihood of finding a job through the classifieds is about 15 to 20 percent. However, if you keep those statistics in mind and adjust the time that you spend on answering advertisements accordingly, the classified advertising of you local newspaper can be an important component of an overall job search program. Use classifieds as a means of determining what kinds of jobs are available. They will give you a sense of who is using DTP as part of their business and what kinds of qualifications they are seeking.

Most companies look for individuals through other means than advertisements. Many jobs are filled in-house through promotion, others come through word-of-mouth referrals. Still others go to prepared individuals who "pound the pavement." This should by no means discourage you. The good news is that there are literally thousands of jobs that are never announced and thousands of companies that are looking for dedicated individuals like yourself. It is a question of learning how to make contact with these companies and marketing your skills, talents, and potential to them.

Use this book to fill yourself in on the opportunities available for individuals who want to use DTP skills. This section will give you some samples of resumes and cover letters that you can alter for your own use. But job hunting is a job in itself and requires dedication, research, and hard work. Make a trip to your library or school's career center and look through some of the excellent books that are available on the mechanics of job searching. Go out and begin talking to individuals who are in the business. Don't be afraid to ask them about what they do and how someone like yourself could become involved with it. You'd be surprised how open and friendly your contacts will be.

TAKE INVENTORY

The first step in a good job search campaign is to inventory your skills. You may be able to do this on your own, but it may be more helpful to sit down and brainstorm with someone who knows you well. You can talk, and your partner can take notes. List your immediate and long-range goals, attitudes toward the work environment, and strengths and weaknesses. Write down all the things that you've done over the years that are even remotely related to your job objective. You'd be surprised at the things that you've done that demonstrate your skills and abilities, even if they weren't necessarily parts of formal job.

If you get stuck, there are many excellent books that will help you inventory your skills and experiences. Richard Bolles' *What Color is Your Parachute?* (10 Speed Press, revised annually) is the bible for many job hunters, and you'll find it at your local library or bookstore. It includes exercises that will help you focus and inventory your skills.

RESEARCH THE MARKET

Use the classified section of your town's or area's Sunday newspaper to get a sense of the market. Try to determine the needs of your area's job market, and begin to formulate how someone like yourself can fit in. Pay special attention to job titles, duties, special needs, and qualifications.

Don't be put off if you don't seem to fit into any of the advertised jobs. Remember that most jobs are unadvertised. Companies consider new employees as investments, and they will often train you to fit their unique requirements.

As an exercise, write an ad that targets someone like yourself. This will help you focus when you put together your resume and cover letter.

Job hunting is a dynamic process, and it is likely that the next few steps in your process can take place simultaneously. Success in this process requires you to be a good sleuth and researcher.

Find Employers

While you keep your eyes on the classified advertisements, you should begin a process of researching companies and networking. Your goal is to find out which companies in your area can utilize someone like yourself. As many of the individuals we've profiled in this book suggest, companies of every size, shape, and industry use desktop publishers, so when you do your research, don't go after just the most obvious choices. Some of the job opportunities are going to be less apparent than others, and you will have to do some digging to find them.

Start at your library or your school's career center. There you will find directories that list companies by industry and the type of employees they hire. Try the Bob Adams Company's Job Bank series which covers employers in the major metropolitan areas. Try also Surrey Books' Insider's Guide series. Titled *How to Get a Job in . . .*, the volumes cover places like Los Angeles, New York, Chicago, Boston, and Atlanta.

Your state is also likely to have a directory that lists companies by industry or service. With careful, judicious use of the telephone, you can begin to find out which companies use desktop publishers and in what capacities. You can also find out who is responsible for hiring desktop publishers within the company.

Set Up Informational Interviews

Once you've found out who's in charge, you should begin to set up informational interviews to become acquainted with the particulars of the companies. These preliminary interviews differ from standard interviews because your goal is strictly to gather information, not to discuss specific positions or promote yourself. You want to meet with as many different employers as you can to find out what their needs are and to determine whether you would like to work for them.

In an informational interview you will approach potential employers, either over the phone or with a letter (see next section) by saying something like: "I'm considering a career that involves desktop publishing and was wondering if you could meet with me to tell me about your job, your company, and how you utilize desktop publishers."

The roles in this kind of interview are reversed. Instead of a company wanting to find out about you, you'll be finding out about the company. Using this approach, you will introduce yourself to a diverse range of potential employers. You may feel nervous about doing this at first, but once you've broken the ice and made your first few contacts, it becomes much easier.

Continue to research jobs *and* companies as an ongoing part of your job-hunting process. When you are out on informational interviews, ask the people you've talked to for recommendations about other companies and individuals to talk to; most will be happy to refer you to friends and colleagues.

You may also want to become part of a local chapter of a professional association or a computer users group. These organizations are likely to be an excellent source of information about local businesses that employ desktop publishers. You are also likely to meet people with similar interests. Check with the organizations listed in Appendix B.

Many of the DTP software companies have extremely loyal followings, and users groups have flourished. You can usually call the software company (many have toll-free numbers) for a referral to a users group in your area. Like the professional associations, these groups can serve as important resources about the local job market.

TARGET A SPECIFIC COMPANY

If you are trying to research a company that has advertised a specific job, call the company's personnel division and request further information about the opening. This will be difficult if the advertised job is part of a blind ad, but many companies won't mind if you call for information, especially if you don't badger them over the phone. If the ad says "No phone calls," *don't* call.

In some cases it might be appropriate to drop by the company offices and collect company literature, speak with public relations staff, and generally ask around.

If a specific company interests you, use the library to further investigate. More and more libraries now carry business, popular, and trade magazines on microfilm. Often you can do a quick search on a company using the library's CD-ROM system. Talk to your librarian about these sources.

The library research and your informational interviews will give you a lot of knowledge about companies and the specifics of jobs. When you eventually meet with someone for a regular interview, you will be a knowledgeable candidate who can ask the right questions.

Keep a journal or log of your job-search process. Track the people you've talked to, companies where you have applied, and advertisements you have answered. The more methodical you are about this process, the more likely you will be to find the right position. Your journal will serve as a valuable memory jogger of who you need to call back and which companies offered the most promising opportunities.

Once you have identified who you want to work for, you will need to put together resumes and cover letters. As a desktop publisher-to-be, you'll want to pay special attention to your letters and resumes because you'll need to adapt to the needs of the marketplace.

Once you've identified the kind of position you want, compile several different versions of your resume and cover letter. If you have access to a computer or word processor, this will become easy. Otherwise it would be wise to use a system at your school's computer lab, your local library, or quick print shop. That way you can update and change your resume as the needs and requirements of each potential job dictate. It may seem easier to use a generic, all-purpose resume and cover letter, but that approach may lessen your chances of being considered for an interview. Whenever possible, tailor each letter and resume to the specific job for which you are applying.

THE COVER LETTER

Letter writing is an important part of any job search campaign, whether you are trying to learn more about a company or actually applying for a job. As a desktop publisher, letters take on an even greater importance because they will be the first place that you demonstrate your style and ability to communicate in printed form. Your cover or query letter is likely to be your means of making a good first impression and interesting the potential employer in pursuing you more seriously.

If your letter is a response to a classified advertisement that is likely to attract many similarly qualified applicants, you will have to find a way to make your letter and resume stand out from the potentially large pool of applicants. Carefully consider your audience. If it's a large corporation or a seemingly conservative smaller company, go with a conservative look and impress them instead with your knowledge of the field and the company. You will distinguish yourself by projecting an image that is knowledgeable, professional, and competent. If the company seems more progressive and bold, tailor your visual approach to suit its image.

It is essential that your cover letter be specific to the job you seek—otherwise you will get lost in the pile. Your letter is an opportunity to elaborate on your qualifications and demonstrate your knowledge of and familiarity with a company and the desktop publishing field in general. Finally, it gives you the chance to request a personal meeting.

Here are some tips.

- *Whenever possible, direct your letter to the person in charge of the hiring.* Your preliminary research should uncover at least this much. Forgo the generic "Dear Sir or Madam," which shows a lack of research. If no name is available—and one cannot be gotten through research—begin with "Dear Human Resources Director" or a similar title.

- *Start your letter with a reference to the specific job and how you have come to apply.* If this is a letter requesting an informational interview, substitute a statement regarding the origin and nature of your interest in the company or program.
- *Focus your letter around the text of the advertisement* when answering a classified advertisement or job posting. Find some way to show how your background suits the listed requirements.
- *Give specific examples* of experience, education, or interests in areas closely linked to the job.
- *Refer to your enclosed resume.* Many writers of cover letters make the mistake of rehashing their resume. Instead, you should use the cover letter to point to elements of your resume that you would like to highlight.
- *Request a meeting in person.* Use the closing section of your letter to request an interview.

Figure 7.1 shows an advertisement that appeared in a local classified ad section, and Figure 7.2 is a job-specific cover letter written in response to that ad. The correspond-

Figure 7.1 Sample Advertisement for DTP Position

Desktop Publisher/Media Specialist. EarthDay New York seeks an energetic desktop publisher for its quarterly magazine. Candidate must be able to work within tight deadlines and handle several projects simultaneously. Contact: Ms. Paullette English, Publisher, EarthDay Resources, 107 Sterling Place, Brooklyn, NY 11217. No calls please.

Figure 7.2 Cover Letter

516 South Albany St.
Ithaca, New York 14850
23 July 1992

Ms. Paullette English
Publisher
EarthDay New York
1007 Sterling Place
Brooklyn, New York 11217

Dear Ms. English:

In the June 27th issue of the *Village Voice* you advertised for an "energetic" desktop publisher to work on your magazine staff. My educational background in communications coupled with my desktop publishing work for not-for-profit, public interest groups indicate my enthusiasm and dedication to environmental issues and my ability to develop and produce effective publications. The enclosed resume highlights my education, training, and experience.

My studies in the communications department at Ithaca College have allowed me to learn the essentials of business communications while allowing me to follow up on my personal interests in the environmental field. Since my arrival, I have developed a solid understanding of the fundamentals of working with print media and have continued to work on my writing and editing skills through coursework in the college's advanced composition program. I will be awarded my B.A. in May 1993—with departmental honors.

While a summer intern for Global Releaf, I had the opportunity to put my desktop publishing and writing skills to work as part of their eco-education program. Global Releaf continues to use my "Radical Reforestation" pamphlet and many of the other collateral materials that I produced for them. My work for City Spirit Publications during the summer of 1989 gave me a firsthand glimpse at the inner workings of the publishing business. As production assistant, I became acquainted with using both Macintosh and Windows software while working as an integral member of a production team.

As the enclosed resume also indicates, I have experience with many of the most popular software packages, and I have exceptional keyboarding skills. More importantly, I have demonstrated the willingness and ability to learn from others and to take the initiative to learn on my own.

I look forward to meeting with your staff to discuss this position. Please call me at your convenience at 607-272-0639 to set up an interview.

Sincerely,

Thomas Wadsworth

ing resume appears in Figure 7.3 later in this chapter. You can use these as starting places for your own versions. Remember that there are many ways to approach your letters and resumes, and you shouldn't feel that you have to fit yourself into any one particular format. Once you've begun the process of meeting with potential employers through informational interviews, you may want to share your resume and cover letter with these decision makers. Ask them for feedback and adjust your work accordingly.

THE RESUME

Author and career expert Richard Bolles likes to play down the importance of resumes, and many of his colleagues in the vocational guidance field agree. Bolles likes to suggest that resumes are nothing more than extended calling cards, and not even good ones at that. He warns that job hunters may put too much emphasis on them. According to Bolles, a good resume can help you get into an interview, but it's not likely to land you the job. The lesson we learn from Bolles is: do your research, talk to the right people, and set yourself up to get the job, then you can use your resume.

You'll want to be ready for that moment, so let's talk about how to put together a resume. We'll review some of the important features, but for more comprehensive instructions on resume writing, consult Yanna Parker's *The*

Damn Good Resume Book (1989, 10 Speed Press) or Jeffrey Allen's *Jeff Allen's Best* (1992, Wiley). Parker's book is especially helpful for desktop publishers because it takes a modern approach and is more sensitive to graphic presentation.

The word *resume* comes from the French and literally means "summary." Many resumes do just that: summarize. But the best resumes will do more. Indeed, your resume should summarize your most important credentials, but it should also focus them so that they meet the requirements of the job that you're after.

As a job hunter, you are now in the marketing and advertising business, but instead of trying to convince consumers to buy your new contraption or eat a great meal at your restaurant, you'll be selling them *you*—that is, your talents and abilities.

There is no single superior resume format. Your resume should be suited to your audience. This section provides samples of the two most popular resume formats: the chronological resume and the functional resume. If you have a lot of work experience in a particular area and have stayed with the same company or several companies for a number of years, use the chronological format. If your background is a hodgepodge of skills and experiences, you may want to go with a functional format.

Regardless of format or sequence, resumes usually provide the same basic information. Make sure to include:

- Name and home address (work address, too, if desired)
- Career or job objectives (match this to requirements of the job you're seeking)
- Educational background
- Paid or volunteer work, and related experience
- Relevant affiliations and licenses, certificates, activities, honors, fluencies (foreign and computer languages)

You can include references on the resume itself, put them on a separate but attached page, or state "References available upon request" on the resume and let the prospective employer who is serious about you ask for them. (The latter approach may save your reference sources from wasting their time talking to people who are only casually interested.)

Do not attach a photograph or include information about your height, weight, race, age, religion, sexual orientation, or marital or family status. It is illegal for a prospective employer to ask for such personal information unless it can be proven relevant to the job, which it can't in most cases. Desktop publishing is unlikely to call for heavy lifting or other such physical capabilities.

Although experts may offer conflicting advice on specific resume format and content, they all agree on language. The attitude that the resume should convey is action. You'll notice that both of our examples rely on strong verbs to communicate the applicants' abilities. Use words like *organized, designed,* and *initiated* when describing your previous work or your competencies.

Figure 7.3 Resume (chronological format)

Thomas Wadsworth
516 South Albany St.
Ithaca, New York 14850
(607) 272-0639

CAREER OBJECTIVE

A position as a desktop publisher/media specialist for a not-for-profit organization advocating environmentally conscious policies.

EDUCATION

Ithaca College, Ithaca, NY
Bachelor of Arts, Communications, expected May 1993

Relevant Coursework

Fundamentals of Graphic Design, Introduction to Electronic Media, Advanced Composition (1 & 2)

EXPERIENCE

Summer Internship
Global Releaf; Washington, DC; Summer 1990

- Designed and developed direct mail campaign for fund-raising campaign
- Typeset and laid out "Radical Reforestation" pamphlet

Production Assistant
City Spirit Publications; Brooklyn, NY; Summer 1989

- Assisted managing editor in layout of annual guidebook using Quark Xpress, Ventura Publisher, and Adobe Illustrator
- Organized and tracked advertising space assignments

RELATED SKILLS

- Proficiency in Windows and Macintosh environments, including: Microsoft Word, Quark Xpress, Adobe Illustrator, Ventura Publisher, and Hijaak
- Exceptional keyboarding skills: 70 wpm

Figure 7.4 Resume (functional format)

DAVIDA JACOBS
932 Ridge Court ○ Evanston, Illinois ○ (708) 869-1782

Objective: A position as a desktop publisher/media specialist for a not-for-profit organization advocating environmentally conscious policies.

HIGHLIGHTS OF QUALIFICATIONS

♦ Outstanding desktop presentation skills (*text and graphics*)
♦ Ability to plan, manage, and follow through on multiple projects
♦ Clear, concise, and engaging writing style
♦ Extensive computer software and hardware experience
♦ Demonstrated commitment to environmentally responsible businesses and organizations

REPRESENTATIVE SKILLS & ACCOMPLISHMENTS

○ Created, designed, and typeset advertisements
○ Typeset and laid out in-house documentation and procedural manual
○ Assisted managing editor in layout of monthly magazine using Quark Xpress, Ventura Publisher, and Adobe Illustrator
○ Copyedited articles; wrote sidebars, captions, and decks

EMPLOYMENT HISTORY

1990 **Assistant Editor**   *Conscious Choices*, Chicago, IL
1989 **Production Assistant**   *Hunter Publications,* Des Plaines, IL

EDUCATION & PROFESSIONAL DEVELOPMENT

B.A., English, Northeastern Illinois University, Chicago, IL
○ Quark Xpress—1 & 2, Microage Computer Centers, Chicago, IL

Keep your resume neat, short, and to the point. As a person who is looking for a job in the desktop publishing field, you should pay particular attention to your design. Don't jam too much onto the page; make judicious use of white space.

It's not necessary to include everything you've ever done. If necessary, cut out information that doesn't seem crucial. It's a good rule not to go more than one page unless you absolutely must.

Always proofread your resume carefully before sending it out. Nothing will handicap you more than a cover letter or resume that has spelling, usage, or grammatical errors, or typos. Have a friend, family member, or teacher read through your correspondence. Finally, keep your resume up-to-date and always have some extra copies around in case someone asks for one.

FOLLOWING UP

Once you've done your research and sent out your cover letter and resume, call the organization to see whether it has received them. Use a professional demeanor when you call. If you have been interviewed, send a personal note to the appropriate person, thanking him or her for the attention and time. You can use the follow-up letter to reinforce something that came up in your interview. It is also an appropriate place to mention relevant information that might not have come up in the interview.

Follow-up calls and thank-you notes are an important part of the process. Even if you don't land a particular job, you'll want to be remembered favorably in the future. Remember, new hires don't always work out. You might not be hired today, but the company may need someone for the same job six months from now. If you like the company and the types of positions it has, find a way to keep in touch. Thank-you notes can be an important part of that process.

TEMPORARY EMPLOYMENT AGENCIES

Perhaps one of the best ways to learn about opportunities in the desktop publishing field is to sign up with a temporary employment agency. These specialized employment services market your talents to many companies on a temporary basis. They arrange the job and take care of all the details, including collecting and paying your salary. In many cases, these agencies also offer health insurance plans, referral bonuses, and other perks as part of the package they offer to workers. The agency does not charge an individual for its services, but instead the business that puts them under contract.

Temp agencies arrange assignments for individuals for as short a period as half a day to as long as a year or more, allowing someone like yourself to try out many different kinds of working situations, often using many different kinds of software and hardware. For a student who is just breaking into the job market, or for the recent graduate who is looking to learn new skills, gain on-the-job experience, and make contacts, temporary agencies are an important resource.

For someone interested in desktop publishing, but without much experience, building a relationship with this type of employment agency can be a critical step in building your credentials. Often these agencies offer free, or inexpensive, training on all kinds of hardware and software. The companies that you are assigned to will sometimes supplement that training as they acclimate you to their own unique requirements. You'll make valuable contacts, often work on top-of-the-line equipment, and learn about the trade by doing it.

For businesses that use temps, it allows the possibility of hiring someone one a trial basis. If they like your work, and it feels like a good match, they might decide to keep you on. Many individuals turn temporary assignments into regular full-time jobs.

Start with your local yellow pages to identify the agencies that serve your area. There are several excellent national agencies that use desktop publishers, including Norrel, Manpower, and Kelly. In your area there are likely to be others, including those that specialize in certain types of businesses, like advertising agencies, publishing houses, or marketing.

When you sign up for a temporary service, the process will be like that of a normal job interview. Be prepared to dress appropriately and professionally. Agencies will usually put you through an extensive screening process, so call ahead to make an appointment. They will likely test your basic office and human relations skills as well as your typing and knowledge of software packages.

Keyboarding skills are especially critical. The speed and accuracy of your typing are likely to have an effect on the kinds of assignments that the temp agency can offer you. Your school or local public library is likely to have computer software that will help you work on your keyboarding skills. If not, there are many excellent books and training programs that you can take out of the library or purchase at your local bookstore. Find a keyboard to practice on, even if it's your Great-aunt Ethel's old Remington manual typewriter.

For desktop publishing positions, it will serve you in good stead to bring along work samples. If you've done any kind of layout or design work, bring along a portfolio. If you haven't, it is always a good idea to prepare these things ahead of time, even if you have to invent projects. (Just make sure you don't try to pass them off as hired work.) School projects are acceptable, and if you're enrolled in a computer or graphic design class or program, consult your teacher or advisor about your portfolio.

If you don't have your own equipment, see if you can use a friend's. Perhaps you can use your school library's or public library's equipment to put together your portfolio. Your town might also have a service like Kinko's that rents computer and laser printer time that will allow you to put together several different kinds of work samples.

Once you get on the assignment, even if it's a short-term one, try to be as observant as possible. It's unethical—and illegal—to take things home with you, but do make mental notes. Try to walk away with some knowledge or skill that you can use on your next assignment. In the desktop publishing field, especially when you are a temp, the more you know about different kinds of software and applications, the more marketable you will be.

Profile: PC Temps

Let's take a closer look at a temporary employment agency that specializes in personal computer work, through the eyes of placement coordinators Timothy Moore and Nancy Honan of Chicago's PC Temps. Their agency represents a new type of service that caters to the specific requirements of electronically oriented offices. Their clients range from small businesses to large multinational corporations. PC Temps is always on the lookout for temps who are competent, flexible, and professional.

PC Temps is the latest offshoot of MAC Temps, a temporary service that was started in the early 1980s by two enterprising Harvard University students who were looking for a way to make money with their computers when they weren't using them for their school work. Their original business was known as Laser Designs, and they started out preparing resumes, flyers, and brochures out of their dorm room for their fellow students and businesses in the Boston area. Slowly they began to expand their range of services so that soon they needed the service of others. Today they have 19 offices around the United States and an office in London.

As an agency that specializes in desktop publishing, PC Temps usually works from a project perspective. Typical projects come from banks, market research firms, graphic design houses, and consumer product manufacturers, but are not necessarily limited by industry. "The PC is so widely used these days in every sector of the business world," says Moore. "We are finding that most companies are trying to do much desktop publishing work in-house, and it often requires them to hire extra personnel to meet the increased work load."

With many companies tightening their belts to deal with difficult economic times, businesses are increasingly relying on firms like PC Temps to provide short-term help to meet a specific need.

Publishing means deadlines, and companies also call on agencies like PC Temps when they are under the gun and need competent, short-term help. "We do lots of manuals and end up sending people out to help with formatting for companies that are under deadline pressure," says Moore. "Our temps typically work with materials that have been created by others. They do formatting work, light editing, and usually apply a predetermined style to a manual or series of manuals—everything from sales and marketing materials to technical documentation."

To be successful at DTP temp work, the individual needs to be able to follow the direction of the client, yet be ready to give input when appropriate. DTP temps, depending on their experience and the needs of the project, might be called on for design input or for feedback. "Our workers usually have solid page layout skills, and these come in handy on the job," says Moore. "When the projects involve the manipulation or creation of graphics, then there is more room for creativity." For the most part, however, temps work within already established parameters.

Aside from manuals and documentation, PC Temps has used DTP-trained workers at law firms working on legal briefs and for businesses that need to develop and create all kinds of forms and applications.

Does an organization like PC Temps look for extensive training in computers and design? Moore says it doesn't always matter. "With DTP it's usually the school of hard knocks," he says. "I don't know that any set training or background is really necessary before someone comes to work for us, though it can't hurt. We have people who have formal schooling in graphic design and they work out fine, but we also have workers who haven't had a day of training in design or in computer graphics."

So what does an organization like PC Temps look for when it hires? "Given our special set of circumstances, we look for flexibility, someone who is looking to do a lot of different kinds of work and who has demonstrated flexibility in the past," Moore says. He and his partner agree that diversity is the key element, and he suggests that students expose themselves to as many different kinds of work environments as they can: "Take as many and all jobs that you can get your hands on so that you can build experience, so that you can get exposure to companies and the way that they do things, different ideas." Temporary services provide the perfect opportunity. "A student fresh out of college will be able to get exposure to small companies and larger companies, and the corporate environment," says Moore's partner, Nancy Honan.

Companies like PC Temps allow students to enjoy transition, as they make career choices or carry out a longer-term job search. "Working for an organization like ours allows the young person who is just entering the job market to get seasoned," Honan says. "One assignment may have them working with one software package, another might have them integrating three packages. Still another might have them work with different kinds of equipment like plotters, scanners, printers. It allows the student to make better choices down the road. You find out what you like to do and what you're good at, whether it is technical documentation or more creative projects."

Moore and Honan see a trend toward skill integration, where more and more companies are trying to build several different types of tasks into one person's job. They advise learning as many different types of computer applications as possible, whether in school, through formal training programs (sometimes offered as part of the adult education program of your local high school or community college), or on your own. "The more fluent you are in various computer applications, the more opportunities that are going to be available to you," Honan advises.

The payment scale varies, depending on the type and complexity of the task involved. For projects that involve DTP skills beyond basic word processing, workers can expect to make from $10 per hour, on the lower end of the scale, to as much as $20 or $35 per hour.

CHAPTER 8

STARTING YOUR OWN BUSINESS

Some of you reading this book may not be excited about the prospect of working for someone else and instead have a bit of entrepreneurial spirit. Remember that desktop publishing has been an entrepreneurial enterprise from the beginning. The developers of the Apple computers that spawned the whole DTP revolution created their first products out of their garages. Freed from the constraints of larger, and perhaps more impersonal companies, many individuals have set up shops in their basements and attics, producing everything from newsletters to resumes to guidebooks. Consult the reading list at the end of this book for further information on running your own DTP business. In Chapter 7 you read a profile of an organization called PC Temps. That business was originally started by a group of college students who used their computers to make some extra money. They were desktop publishers who helped their fellow students put together resumes. Business was so

117

good that they began to branch out into providing their services to companies.

While starting a business may not be something that you are financially equipped to do, there are many ways to get started that require little or no outlay of money. If you are ambitious, you can get a good start, and your resourcefulness just might give you an edge on the competition.

Equipment and know-how are likely to be your first stumbling blocks, but these can be overcome. You may have parents, siblings, or friends who have the equipment and software you need to get started in learning about DTP. A good library will have a varied selection of manuals and books on design and software. Your school's computer lab or your local library may also have equipment that will allow you to get started. Some local quickprint shops like the nationally franchised Kinko's chain rent computer and laser print time. Soon enough you, too, may be making extra cash preparing flyers, brochures, business cards, resumes, and announcements.

If running your own DTP business seems too consuming for you, but the idea of working out of your home is attractive, you'll be interested in the next section on telecommuting, one of the revolutionary ways of doing business that includes a growing number of desktop publishers.

TELECOMMUTING, SELF-PUBLISHING, AND INDEPENDENT DESKTOP PUBLISHING BUSINESSES

Myriad opportunities have become available for self-employed individuals and small businesses, many of which are now publishing books and every shape and size document out of home offices, basements, or small shops. DTP allows anyone with access to a personal computer to broadcast a message. From guidebooks, to books of poetry, to comic books, to brochures, to posters and fliers, to invitations, to business cards, the possibilities are enormous. One company announced that it has developed a system to produce imprints for T-shirts using the designs created on clients' personal computers. All you need is a relatively inexpensive piece of software, access to a laser printer, and some special paper—and you're ready to go.

There is a DTP product called "Freedom of the Press," a name that is more appropriate than one might think on initial inspection. More and more companies are allowing their staff members to work out of their homes, and more and more creative entrepreneurs are starting at-home businesses. In the early 1990s more than 35 million Americans worked at home, either part time or full time, and the numbers are growing. Let's meet one of these enterprising individuals.

Profile: Jill Simone

Jill Simone has been a writer, editor, and desktop publisher since 1987. As staff editor for the New York City-based music distribution and marketing company Sound Traveller, Simone is responsible for the monthly compilation of the company's subscriber-based newsletter. Like the rest of the staff, when Simone was hired, she came to the company's Brooklyn offices daily and went about her work: making phone calls, writing, and desktop-publishing newsletters, marketing pieces, and books. Every month she developed and laid out the newsletter on the office's computer system.

From the newsletter's beginning in 1990, Simone says, the staff always used DTP. "I wasn't trained in traditional graphic arts," she explains. "I learned my trade right on the computer—everything from the writing, to editing, to layout—so when we started the newsletter, there was no question as to how we were going to go about doing it." She worked closely with Chris Haynes, the marketing manager, working with the newsletter copy that he wrote and the informational blurbs and marketing materials that the record companies supplied to them.

Sound Traveller is dedicated to the specialized alternative and new age music markets. Simone's boss, Toni Santodonato, depends on her knowledge and experience with these materials and her expert knowledge of the company's production process.

When Simone approached her boss last fall and explained that she would be moving to the Midwest, Santodonato was concerned about the disruption that a change in staff would cause and was worried about finding a suitable replacement. To add to Santodonato's difficulties, Haynes wanted to move to the Pioneer Valley in Massachusetts so that he could have more time to pursue his own musical composition.

Simone proposed a solution that would enable her and Haynes to continue working on the publication, while allowing them both to go ahead with their moving plans. Simone and Haynes both had their own personal computers with modems, so they convinced Santodonato to purchase a modem and software that would allow them to communicate directly with the office.

With the new computer equipment in place, Haynes continues to compile the newsletter copy out of his at-home office in Amherst. Simone receives the copy electronically over the phone lines. She edits it, adds whatever special features they will be running that month, and finally lays out the copy in her office. Finally, on deadline, she has her computer call Sound Traveller's office computer after business hours and, by using a special remote computing program, she transmits the fully laid-out newsletter to New York. When Santodonato arrives in the office the following day, she prints out the final copy. If minor changes need to be made, the in-house Sound Traveller staff keys them directly in the office system. If there are more substantial changes to be made, Santodonato faxes a marked-up copy back to Simone for revisions.

"The first time Chris and I did the newsletter this way, we couldn't believe what was happening," Simone says. "We were more than a thousand miles away from each other and yet we were able to continue to collaborate. We both were laughing the whole time."

Santodonato is happy with this arrangement, too. She is able to maintain the high quality of her publication and save money in the process. Because Haynes and Simone now charge her a flat fee for their services as independent contractors, she can budget her newsletter accordingly and not incur the expense of having two in-house employees.

"Only a few short years ago this would not have been possible," says Simone. "I'm glad that I can continue to work with Chris and Toni, and now I can do that out of my home office, or on the road somewhere."

The new arrangement has also allowed Simone to work for several clients simultaneously. Sound Traveller is only one example of the possibilities for telecommuters, and the next decade will see more and more people doing work out of their homes.

CHAPTER 9

FUTURE TRENDS

What does the future hold for desktop publishing? No one knows for sure, but this author suspects that the sky's the limit. The technology and its applications have grown so quickly, and over such a short period, it is difficult to predict what will come next.

Some things, however, are certain. The software and hardware will continue to get more powerful and easier to use. By the mid-1990s, we can expect to see even the simplest offices equipped with computers and peripherals that are capable of producing sophisticated documents. More and more individuals will be called upon as part of their work to produce these printed materials. With that in mind, let's daydream about some future trends.

DTP AND THE PRINTING TRADES

For the most part, since DTP's inception, desktop publishing and the printing trades have had a somewhat uneasy working relationship. When upstart desktop publishers showed up with their computers and laser printers, the printing trades felt threatened. Many DTP publishers were good at handling the technology, but less adept at design, typography, and the nuances of taking an idea all the way to the printed page. The printing trades worried about competition and a dilution of quality.

Prior to the mid-1980s, printers had been controlling print media since Gutenberg's development of the printing press 500 years earlier. The printing trades were long of tradition and pride. They did not take the coming of desktop publishing lightly. The prevailing industry belief was that desktop publishers could never produce materials with the same quality or elegance that the printing trades could do through traditional means. Desktop publishers were a thorn in their side, taking away business and threatening their absolute control over the production of printed materials. It was not an easy issue to resolve.

But desktop publishing was too good a technology to ignore for too long, even if it required the printing trades to rethink many of the ways that they go about things. In the short years since DTP arrival, the printing industry has learned, although begrudgingly at first, to work with desktop publishers. Furthermore, the printing trades have begun to embrace the technology themselves.

The next decade will see further integration as DTP practitioners and printers learn how to better interface with each other. One of the first outcomes is that desktop publishers will be able to send their work to printers in other formats aside from mechanicals. The work of traditional typesetters and that of desktop publishers is on the road to becoming indistinguishable. Already many desktop publishers are outputting their work to film, bypassing part of the offset printing process and thus saving time and money and improving the relative sharpness of the resulting printed pages. Desktop publishers of the future are likely to send their work electronically to their printers.

What this means to the author, publisher, or business is far more control over the appearance of their work. It also means that an individual with printing needs will be able to produce printed pages at a fair price with a very quick turnaround. While many desktop publishing jobs have been created outside the traditional printing industry, job seekers can expect to find work as desktop publishers within traditional printing organizations. They can also expect many of the traditional printing tasks, like color separation, to become computerized and DTP-oriented.

COLOR

That more and more of the desktop publishing of the future will be in color is not a question. How quickly it will become part of our day-to-day work is the much more relevant query. All the major software publishers are working on color enhancements to their products, providing desktop publishers with unprecedented control over the final appearance of their printed work.

Individuals are now able to produce full-color work on their desktops, and as full-color printing becomes cheaper and more accessible, more and more desktop publishers will include color work as part of their repertoire. In 1992 the price of color laser printers was still out of the range of most smaller practitioners of DTP, but as with all other aspects of the technology, the price is sure to come down rapidly.

Shifting to color will not be as simple as purchasing the appropriate hardware and software. People who specialize in techniques like color separation spend years learning the subtleties of transferring their color concepts to paper. The manipulation of color adds other degrees of complexity to the desktop publishing process that will require users to have additional training and aptitude. Still, those with talent and instincts would be wise to learn about color and color manipulation.

IMAGE PROCESSING

More and more of the opportunities in the DTP field require the ability to process not only text, but also images. Image processing is a capability that allows desktop publishers an unlimited set of new creative possibilities. It is an area that is sure to require skilled individuals in the years to come.

Image processing allows the DTP user to manipulate and combine graphic images created on the desktop personal computer with photographs, art, and images from other sources. With the improvement and proliferation of scanners and peripherals like digital cameras, image processing is becoming an integral part of many desktop publishers' work.

Just consider the possibilities of a desktop publisher who uses a digital camera. He or she goes out and shoots a photograph, but instead of passing along the film to a processing laboratory, the image is recorded on a silicon chip. Back at the desktop, the images are then processed with software instead of chemicals. In their digital format, the images are then manipulated in many of the same ways that can happen in a traditional darkroom. Enlargements, reductions, enhancements are all elementary. Similarly, techniques like solarization or negative imaging are also available with a few clicks on the mouse or strokes on the keyboard. The image is then easily and quickly transferred into the DTPer's newsletter, book chapter, or flyer without the need of outside professionals.

NEW FORMATS

Likely to change in the next decade are the formats in which we deliver information. Electronic publishing of every kind—from CD-ROM (Compact Disc-Read Only Memory), to newspapers and newsletters delivered by fax machines, to on-line electronic publications—is beginning to change the way that we use and process information. Technology is likely to free up our dependence on paper, with all of its associated negative environmental side effects. Paper publications will exist, but they will not be our predominant method of communicating. Individuals like yourself will be creating, manipulating, and producing this information on their desktops. This will be DTP, but it will be a DTP that is far more sophisticated and dynamic.

MULTIMEDIA

As the name implies, multimedia allows the desktop computer user to meld together many different kinds of media, including music, voice, and animation, and allows reproduction on a desktop computer. Multimedia gives the desktop computer user the capabilities of a film or video producer. It allows for the presentation and creation of sophisticated publications that are dynamic and present material in new and unusual ways. Close at hand are talking magazines, as well as encyclopedias and publications that integrate information, film clips, musical pieces, and every kind of other imaginable media.

The everyday use of multimedia is already here for many in the business and educational world, but whether individuals will commonly produce in this format is another story. The production of these materials requires an equipment outlay that will make it inaccessible for all but the well-to-do for many years. Additionally, this technology requires the producer to acquire a much higher level of training than is normally required by the typical desktop publisher.

INDUSTRY STANDARDS

As with any new field, DTP in its first decade has experienced a struggle to develop standards. For the first few years, most users were broken down into camps. There were the "Macintosh people," the "IBM people," and the "Unix/mainframe people." Typically desktop publishers would learn a system and its associated tools and in turn steadfastly refuse to acknowledge the importance and worthiness of competing formats.

The early 1990s have shown a movement toward the development of uniform standards, so that individuals can communicate and share information with users of competing systems. Computer giants Apple and IBM, once bitter foes, signed an agreement to share technology and cooperate in the development of new technology.

As more and more software publishers make their packages available in different system formats, the division between operating systems is likely to further diminish. It will become much easier for someone to move from one system of software package to another, allowing them to transfer the skills in the process.

A FINAL WORD

Desktop publishing is a very fast-moving field. For that reason, this book has focused on the people who use the technology, rather than the technology itself. Get a subscription to one of the many fine magazines listed in Appendix C of this book if you want the most up-to-date information about the latest developments in hardware and software.

The technology has come a long way since its humble beginnings in the mid-1980s, and it continues to grow at a lightning pace. Today's desktop publishers work on systems that are hundreds of times more powerful, and infinitely easier to use, than their counterparts of only a few years ago. And it gets more powerful and easier all the time. It's hard to believe that the field is still so young.

Opportunities in Desktop Publishing has explored the many different kinds of individuals and businesses that use desktop publishing. And what is presented here is only a small sampling, because the possibilities are really endless.

The strength of desktop publishing is in its ability to allow individuals to use the power of information without having to pay a premium price for it. It has allowed everybody from secretaries to artists to executives to share their work in a high-quality format with others, and it allows them to do it in a timely fashion.

Whether you choose to work in one of the many capacities outlined in this book, or whether you choose to start up one of the many enterprising small businesses that are using desktop publishing, DTP offers a powerful set of tools to the individual. I encourage you to participate in this new "freedom of the press." It's yours to use.

RECOMMENDED READING

Barry, John A., and Frederic E. Davis. *Desktop Publishing, IBM Edition.* Homewood, Ill.: Dow Jones-Irwin, 1988.

Blatner, David. *Desktop Publishers Survival Kit.* Berkeley, Calif.: Peachpit Press, 1992.

Borowsky, Irwin J. *Opportunities in Printing Careers.* Lincolnwood, Ill.: VGM Career Horizons, 1992.

Bove, Tony, et al. *The Art of Desktop Publishing.* New York: Bantam Books, 1990.

Burke, Clifford. *Type from the Desktop: Designing with Type and Your Computer.* Chapel Hill, N.C.: Ventana Press, 1990.

Chappell, Warren. *A Short History of the Printed Word.* New York: Alfred A. Knopf, 1970.

Eckhart, Robert C. et al. *Desktop Publishing Secrets.* Berkeley, Calif.: Peachpit Press, 1992.

Edwards, Paul. *Working from Home: Everything You Need to Know About Living and Working Under the Same Roof.* Los Angeles: J. P. Tarcher.

Felici, James. *How to Get Great Type Out of Your Computer.* Cincinnati, Ohio: North Light Books, 1992.

Kamoroff, Bernard. *Small Time Operator: How to Start Your Own Small Business, Keep Your Books, Pay Your Taxes & Stay Out of Trouble: A Guide and Workbook.* Laytonville, Calif.: Bell Springs, 1989.

Kleper, Michael L. *The Illustrated Handbook of Desktop Publishing and Typesetting.* Blue Ridge Summit, Penn.: TAB Professional and Reference Books, 1990.

Kramer, Felix, and Maggie Lovaas. *Desktop Publishing Success: How to Start and Run a Desktop Publishing Business.* Homewood, Ill.: Business One Irwin, 1991.

Kvern, Olav Martin, and Stephen Roth. *Real World Pagemaker: Industrial Strength Techniques.* New York: Bantam Books, 1990.

Manouses, Stephen, and Scott Tilden. *The Professional Look: The Complete Guide to Desktop Publishing.* San Jose: Venture Perspective Press, 1990.

Meyer, John. *Ventura Publisher DOS/GEM Edition: Reference Guide.* San Diego: Xerox Corp. 1989.

Parker, Roger. *Looking Good in Print: A Guide to Basic Design for Desktop Publishing.* Chapel Hill, N.C.: Ventana Press, 1990.

————. *The Makeover Book: 101 Design Solutions for Desktop Publishing.* Chapel Hill, N.C.: Ventana Press, 1989.

Schepp, Brad. *The Telecommuter's Handbook: How to Work for a Salary Without Ever Leaving the House.* New York: Pharos Books, 1990.

Shushan, Ronnie. *Desktop Publishing by Design.* Redmond, Wash.: Microsoft Press, 1991.

White, Jan V. *Great Pages: A Common-Sense Approach to Effective Desktop Design.* El Segundo, Calif.: Serif Publishing, 1988.

Williams, Robin. *Jargon: An Informal Computer Dictionary.* Berkeley, Calif.: Peachpit Press, 1992.

———. *The PC is Not a Typewriter.* Berkeley, Calif.: Peachpit Press, 1992.

Williams, Thomas A. *How to Make $100,000 a Year in Desktop Publishing.* White Hall, Va.: Betterway, 1990.

PROFESSIONAL ORGANIZATIONS AND ASSOCIATIONS

Association for the Development of
Electronic Publishing Techniques
360 N. Michigan Avenue
Chicago, IL 60601
Phone (312) 609-0577

Association for Desktop Publishers
P.O. Box 881667
San Diego, CA 92168-1667
Phone (619) 563-9714

Dynamic Graphics Educational Foundation
6000 N. Forest Park Drive
Peoria, IL 61614-3592
Phone (309) 688-8866

Graphics Arts Technical Foundation (GATF)
4615 Forbes Avenue
Pittsburgh, PA 15213
Phone (412) 621-6941

National Association for Desktop Publishers
  Museum Wharf
  300 Congress Street
  Boston, MA 02210
  Phone (617) 426-2885

Seybold Seminars
  29160 Healthcliff Rd., Suite 2000
  P.O. Box 578
  Malibu, CA 90265-0578
  Phone (310) 457-8500

XPLOR International
  The Association for
  Electronic Printing Professionals
  P.O. Box 1501
  2550 Via Tejon, Suite 3L
  Palos Verdes Estates, CA 90274
  Phone (800) 669-7567

MAGAZINES AND TRADE
PUBLICATIONS

Desktop Communications
  P.O. Box 94175
  Atlanta, GA 30341

Desktop Publisher
  P.O. Box 3200
  Maple Glen, PA 19002

PC Publishing
  P.O. Box 5050
  Des Plaines, IL 60605

Personal Publishing
  P.O. Box 3019
  Wheaton, IL 60189

Publish
  P.O. Box 51966
  Boulder, CO 80321

GLOSSARY

ASCII (American Standard Code for Information Interchange). A standardized computer format that can be shared by many different types of computers and systems, regardless of the brand or style. Information stored in this format doesn't have any variation to it: there are no bold letters, no italics; it is just straight text.

Bit-Mapped Computer Graphics. When you convert a photograph or drawing into a computer format, the process breaks down the image into little dots, or *bits*. This is a similar process to what newspaper and book publishers use to print photographs. Desktop publishers often use devices like scanners to convert already printed material into a bit-map. Drawing and painting software will also convert computer-generated art or graphics into a bit-map so that it can be integrated with text.

CD-ROM (Compact Disc-Read Only Memory). A digital format that allows the storage and retrieval of information on a laser disc. A single compact disc is capable of holding the equivalent of 300,000 pages of written text. CD-ROM players are becoming integral parts of personal computers because they have much less size and speed limitation than conventional magnetic storage devices like floppy discs or hard drives.

Camera-ready.   Any piece of text or graphics, whether computer- or hand-generated, that is ready to be printed. Most current printing involves literally taking a photograph of camera-ready pages, and then using the film to reproduce the final copies.

Clip art.   A term that desktop publishing borrows from the traditional graphic art world to describe ready-made artwork, symbols, or icons that people can purchase for incorporation into their publications. Traditionally these designs came in books so that people could clip them out and paste them into their documents. Today clip art is available in digital computer form. Many desktop publishers purchase this art in a compact disc (CD) format; thousands of different images can be stored and cataloged on a single CD.

Color separation.   The process by which color images (photograph, artwork, or computer file) that are used in color printing are converted into their primary component colors so that they can be transferred to composite film for printing. Color separation is a highly refined skill, and success in this process requires training and considerable practice. More and more color separation work is taking place on desktop computers.

CRT (Cathode Ray Tube). A term that is becoming dated. Refers to the monitor or terminal upon which computer users display their work. Televisions are also CRTs. Sometimes also referred to as *VDT* (Video Display Terminal).

Daisy wheel. Before laser printers, many computer printers utilized this type of impact process for printouts. It comes out of the more advanced typewriters that predated the personal computer revolution. They produced type-writer-quality print using raised letters arranged on a wheel that struck a ribbon. The printing quality of these printers was very good for letters, but it was extraordinarily slow by today's standards.

Desktop publishing (DTP). The ability to produce camera-ready, reproduction-quality pages or publications that integrate words and pictures using a personal computer or computer terminal.

Dot-matrix. A style of computer printing that relies on pins that strike a ribbon to create characters or graphics. The name comes from the dots that are arranged to form letters. Technology has improved considerably since the introduction of dot-matrix printers in the late 1970s. Though they are still common, these printers are not used by serious desktop publishers for anything more than rough drafts of proofs. Compared to that of laser printers or daisy wheels, their type is hard to read.

DPI.   (Dots Per Inch). A measure that rates the relative sharpness of a printout, based on the actual number of dots in a given inch of print. The higher the number, the sharper the resolution.

DTP.   Desktop publishing.

Font.   A complete collection of letters, figures, symbols, punctuation, and special characters that belong to the same type family and have the same size and weight (thickness).

Graphics.   Any element that makes up a printed page that is not strictly text, including photographs, line-art, tables, graphs, and charts.

Impact printer.   See *Dot-matrix*.

Laser printer.   A printing device that uses technology similar to that of a photocopy machine. As the name implies, it uses a laser to reproduce the pages that you generate on your computer. What separates laser printers from impact (dot-matrix) printers is their ability to produce printouts that are camera-ready at high resolution (able to show sharp detail). Laser printers typically have their own computer on board to translate the information that your software generates. Laser printers typically print at 300 DPI (dots per inch) and have the ability to reproduce graphics and many different type styles.

Letterpress. One of the oldest forms of printing reproduction that is still in use. This method involves a printer choosing type for each letter that makes up the printout and placing it together to form the page. Ink is then applied to the type and the type is exposed to the paper. The name is derived from the literal process of the letters pressing against the paper.

Line art. Traditionally this referred to illustrations or pictures that artists produced that were made up of only black and white tones with no shades of gray. In computer terminology, this refers to computer-generated drawings that are stored mathematically.

Modem. A computer device that allows the transmission of computer information over the phone lines.

Pasteup. A page assembled for publication through traditional means. A pasteup artist literally cuts and pastes page elements like photographs, drawings, and text onto boards that are sent to a printer for reproduction.

Photoengraving. A more modern form of printing than the letterpress that uses plates that are cast or engraved and onto which ink is applied.

PostScript. A computer language used to describe how to print a page that consists of both text and pictures. Originally developed by the Adobe Corporation for use with the original Apple MacIntosh LaserWriter printers, it is becoming the universal printer language for desktop publishers regardless of the brand or style of computer. Files that are output using PostScript can be printed on any printer that uses PostScript. The name comes from the fact that much of the computer processing required for the printout takes place after the computer sends the printer the information.

Proportional spacing.   Different space is given to each letter or character, so that the letter *i* gets a smaller amount of space than does the letter *M*. This is what separates typewritten documents from typeset documents. It gives computer users the ability to mimic traditional printers.

Scanner.   A device that converts a paper drawing into a computer image. Scanners are paperless copy machines that allow a desktop publisher to incorporate graphics alongside the text. They are also capable of capturing printed images. Scanned text can be converted to computer word processing format with the aid of optical character recognition (OCR) software.

Screening.   A technique used in the printing of photographs or art that converts them into a series of dots.

Typeface.   Refers to a name given to the style of type. Among the most common are Times Roman and Helvetica.

WYSIWYG   (What You See Is What You Get). Refers to the ability to display on the computer screen a close representation of what will be printed. The Apple Macintosh computer systems were the first commercially available examples of this feature, though most sophisticated computer software now has this capability. The development of WYSIWYG-style software was an essential element in the advancement of desktop publishing because it allowed an individual to compose pages right on the computer screen.

VGM CAREER BOOKS

OPPORTUNITIES IN
*Available in both paperback and
  hardbound editions*
Accounting
Acting
Advertising
Aerospace
Agriculture
Airline
Animal and Pet Care
Architecture
Automotive Service
Banking
Beauty Culture
Biological Sciences
Biotechnology
Book Publishing
Broadcasting
Building Construction Trades
Business Communication
Business Management
Cable Television
Carpentry
Chemical Engineering
Chemistry
Child Care
Chiropractic Health Care
Civil Engineering
Cleaning Service
Commercial Art and Graphic Design
Computer Aided Design and
  Computer Aided Mfg.
Computer Maintenance
Computer Science
Counseling & Development
Crafts
Culinary
Customer Service
Dance
Data Processing
Dental Care
Direct Marketing
Drafting
Electrical Trades
Electronic and Electrical Engineering
Electronics
Energy
Engineering
Engineering Technology
Environmental
Eye Care
Fashion
Fast Food
Federal Government
Film
Financial
Fire Protection Services
Fitness
Food Services
Foreign Language
Forestry
Gerontology
Government Service
Graphic Communications
Health and Medical
High Tech
Home Economics
Hospital Administration
Hotel & Motel Management
Human Resources Management
  Careers
Information Systems
Insurance
Interior Design
International Business
Journalism
Laser Technology
Law

Law Enforcement and Criminal Justice
Library and Information Science
Machine Trades
Magazine Publishing
Management
Marine & Maritime
Marketing
Materials Science
Mechanical Engineering
Medical Technology
Metalworking
Microelectronics
Military
Modeling
Music
Newspaper Publishing
Nursing
Nutrition
Occupational Therapy
Office Occupations
Opticianry
Optometry
Packaging Science
Paralegal Careers
Paramedical Careers
Part-time & Summer Jobs
Performing Arts
Petroleum
Pharmacy
Photography
Physical Therapy
Physician
Plastics
Plumbing & Pipe Fitting
Podiatric Medicine
Postal Service
Printing
Property Management
Psychiatry
Psychology
Public Health
Public Relations
Purchasing
Real Estate
Recreation and Leisure
Refrigeration and Air Conditioning
Religious Service
Restaurant
Retailing
Robotics
Sales
Sales & Marketing
Secretarial
Securities
Social Science
Social Work
Speech-Language Pathology
Sports & Athletics
Sports Medicine
State and Local Government
Teaching
Technical Communications
Telecommunications
Television and Video
Theatrical Design & Production
Transportation
Travel
Trucking
Veterinary Medicine
Visual Arts
Vocational and Technical
Warehousing
Waste Management
Welding
Word Processing
Writing
Your Own Service Business

CAREERS IN Accounting; Advertising;
Business; Communications; Computers;
Education; Engineering; Health Care;
High Tech; Law; Marketing; Medicine;
Science

CAREER DIRECTORIES
Careers Encyclopedia
Dictionary of Occupational Titles
Occupational Outlook Handbook

CAREER PLANNING
Admissions Guide to Selective
  Business Schools
Career Planning and Development for
  College Students and Recent
  Graduates
Careers Checklists
Careers for Animal Lovers
Careers for Bookworms
Careers for Culture Lovers
Careers for Foreign Language
  Aficionados
Careers for Good Samaritans
Careers for Gourmets
Careers for Nature Lovers
Careers for Numbers Crunchers
Careers for Sports Nuts
Careers for Travel Buffs
Guide to Basic Resume Writing
Handbook of Business and
  Management Careers
Handbook of Health Care Careers
Handbook of Scientific and
  Technical Careers
How to Change Your Career
How to Choose the Right Career
How to Get and Keep
  Your First Job
How to Get into the Right Law School
How to Get People to Do Things
  Your Way
How to Have a Winning Job Interview
How to Land a Better Job
How to Make the Right Career Moves
How to Market Your College Degree
How to Prepare a *Curriculum Vitae*
How to Prepare for College
How to Run Your Own Home Business
How to Succeed in Collge
How to Succeed in High School
How to Write a Winning Resume
Joyce Lain Kennedy's Career Book
Planning Your Career of Tomorrow
Planning Your College Education
Planning Your Military Career
Planning Your Young Child's
  Education
Resumes for Advertising Careers
Resumes for College Students & Recent
  Graduates
Resumes for Communications Careers
Resumes for Education Careers
Resumes for High School Graduates
Resumes for High Tech Careers
Resumes for Sales and Marketing Careers
Successful Interviewing for College
  Seniors

SURVIVAL GUIDES
Dropping Out or Hanging In
High School Survival Guide
College Survival Guide

 **VGM Career Horizons**
a division of NTC *Publishing Group*
4255 West Touhy Avenue
Lincolnwood, Illinois 60646-1975